Ministry of Education & Training
13th Floor, Mowat Block, Queen's Park
Toronto, Ontario M7A 1L2

Missing Pieces III

AN ALTERNATIVE GUIDE TO CANADIAN POST-SECONDARY EDUCATION

Edited by
**Denise Doherty-Delorme
and Erika Shaker**

CANADIAN CENTRE FOR POLICY ALTERNATIVES
March 2002

PRINTED IN CANADA

Table of contents

Acknowledgements i
Contributors iii
Missing Pieces III: Introduction 1
Provincial rankings 7
Newfoundland & Labrador 12
Prince Edward Island 16
Nova Scotia Overview 19
New Brunswick 22
Performing for the market in Quebec 24
What are the Ontario government's policy directions concerning higher education? ..27
Manitoba 35
Post-secondary education in Saskatchewan 41
Higher education in Alberta, 2001-2002 45
British Columbia 48
Confronting the higher education debates 52
Education and human capital 63
Access to education and training 67
Increasing the burden: Student financial assistance in Canada 76
Audit:Trent University 85
University finance in Canada: Into the 21st century 88
What is a high quality education? 94
Dumbing down distance education: The corporate agenda and the end of quality 99
Post September 11 afterword 104
The university as a workplace in the global context 107
Big biotech buys the building: Students and faculty confront big money and corporate
    science on campus 122
University competition: New trouble in the making 128
Excerpt from women's economic independence and security: A federal/provincial/
    territorial strategic framework 133
Resisting casualization: Contract academic staff mobilize 136
Appendix 140

Acknowledgements

We would like to thank all those who contributed to the completion of this report: the students, faculty, support staff, researchers, writers and editors who freely gave of their time, support and expertise. Once again we are privileged to work with such a dedicated group of individuals and organizations that continue to strive for a system of higher education that serves the needs of all Canadians: we look forward to continuing to work with you.

We would also like to express our vast appreciation to the staff of the Canadian Centre for Policy Alternatives: Melanie Allison, Paul Leduc Browne, Ansky Espinoza, Scott Sinclair, Diane Touchette, CCPA-BC, CCPA-MB and CCPA-NS. We would also like to thank Bruce Campbell, Ed Finn and Kerri-Anne Finn for their patience, advice and expertise throughout this work.

A number of supporting organizations and individuals deserve special mention: the Canadian Federation of Students, the Canadian Association of University Teachers, the Canadian Labour Congress, and the Canadian Union of Public Employees for their tireless work in support of Canadian higher education; Ian Boyko, Ron Melchers and David Robinson for their advice and assistance; Gord McWilliams and Laurie Poon of Studio 2 Graphic Design; and Transcontinental Printing.

Finally, we would like to thank our families for their support, advice and understanding throughout this project.

The Editors.

About the editors: Denise Doherty-Delorme is a CCPA Research Associate. Erika Shaker is Director of the CCPA Education Project.

Contributors

Bob Baldwin
National Director of Social and Economic Policy Department
Canadian Labour Congress

David Bernans
Researcher, Concordia Student Union and author of *Con U Inc.: Privatization, Marketization and Globalization at Concordia University (and beyond)*

Liz Blackwell
Researcher, Trent Central Student Association, Trent University

Michael Conlon
Researcher, National Office, Canadian Federation of Students

Denise Doherty-Delorme
Research Associate, Canadian Centre for Policy Alternatives

Chris Dooley
Independent Scholar, Canadian Centre for Policy Alternative (MB) Research Associate

Pam Frache
Campaigns and Government Relations Co-ordinator, Canadian Federation of Students (ON)

Cameron Graham
Faculty of Management, University of Calgary

Theresa Healy
Researcher, Canadian Union of Public Employees

John McMurtry
Professor of Philosophy, University of Guelph

Ron Melchers
Department of Criminology, University of Ottawa

Roseanne Moran
Communications & Research, College Institute Educators' Association of BC

Dean Neu
Professor of Accounting and Educational Finance, University of Alberta

David Noble
Department of History, York University

James M. Pitsula
Department of History, University of Regina

Claire Polster
Department of Sociology, University of Regina

Mark Rosenfeld
Director of Research, Ontario Confederation of University Faculty Associations

Theresa C. Sabourin
Maritimes Organiser, Canadian Federation of Students

Todd Scarth
Director, Manitoba Office, Canadian Centre for Policy Alternatives

Erika Shaker
Director, CCPA Education Project, Canadian Centre for Policy Alternatives

Lucy Sharratt
Researcher, Polaris Institute

Vicky Smallman
Professional Officer, Canadian Association of University Teachers

Jennifer Sumner
School of Rural Extension Studies, University of Guelph

Michael Temelini
Department of Political Science, Concordia University

Anita Zaenker
National Executive Representative, Canadian Federation of Students (BC)

Missing Pieces III: Introduction

By Denise Doherty-Delorme and Erika Shaker

This is the third edition of *Missing Pieces*. As with earlier versions, we have attempted to provide a broader context for the examination of issues surrounding the state of higher education in Canada. We have continued to focus on the defining principles of post-secondary education: quality, equity, accessibility/affordability/opportunity, and public accountability. These principles are defined, as in previous editions of *Missing Pieces*, as follows:

Equity

Equity is defined as comprising those mechanisms in place at a provincial level to ensure that all students, regardless of gender, place of origin, or socioeconomic status, can make optimal use of higher education in whichever location and discipline they choose.

It also requires that those opportunities not only be protected, but also reinforced and thoroughly integrated into every aspect of higher education. It also refers to the facilitation of full participation in the higher education experience by all members of the post-secondary community—students as well as faculty, support staff and administration.

Accessibility, affordability and opportunity

We have defined accessibility (including affordability and opportunity) as the freedom to obtain and make use of a post-secondary education. It provides an examination of the financial measures in place to ensure that students are able to afford to attend the university or college of their choice, to complete their education, and have the opportunity to use that education upon graduation. The accessibility ranking is determined largely by how the provinces have participated in eliminating—or at least mitigating—financial barriers to university and college.

Quality

We have defined quality as the degree of excellence of the entire educational experience. A high-quality education depends on the provincial and federal governments' commitment to fostering a well-rounded educational experience and environment. In part, this includes: the quality of student life;

the adequacy of university or college finances; the breadth of disciplines and modes of learning offered; and student access to tenured faculty.

Public accountability

Accountability is defined as the degree to which provincial governments ensure that universities and colleges are in fact accountable to the public, and not to corporations or individual sponsors or clients. In addition, it means that universities and colleges, and their functions of teaching, research and community service, remain in the public domain and are not privatized. This is determined largely by the amount of public funding dedicated to post-secondary education budgets as compared to funding from private donations or student fees, which download the cost of education to individuals. We also include in this category the degree to which governments have demonstrated accountability to all age groups in their pursuit of higher education.

Missing Pieces is aimed at provincial and federal education policy-makers, but it reflects the voices of students, faculty, support staff, and Canadian citizens. Using publicly available data, mostly from Statistics Canada, *Missing Pieces* grades and ranks the provinces on their commitment to higher education, teaching, scholarly work, and research. In addition, this report provides contextual research papers that support a more in-depth look at the situation than can be presented in a simple ranking.

Missing Pieces has chosen to compare the provinces, not individual institutions, for a number of reasons. Other rankings that compare individual schools or look only at one specific area are too arbitrary or too limited to be of much use to policy-makers, and cannot be used in any meaningful way to plan for the future. The federal and provincial governments control the funding and set out the policies for higher education. College and university administrators must work within the confines of these policies and budgets in order to meet the needs of their students and staff, and, more broadly, the public that these institutions ultimately serve.

As shown in previous editions of *Missing Pieces*[1], the province where a student lives and is educated unfortunately has a significant impact on his or her opportunity to study and to further contribute to society. Unfortunate, because in a democratic society equality of opportunity to education should be guaranteed, established and safeguarded. While cutbacks in transfer payments by the federal government have had a serious effect on all areas of post-secondary education (PSE), provincial governments have provided varying levels of support for higher education, without any real national consistency. This has evolved into a patchwork quilt of higher education policies that differ from province to province. Today, more than ever, a student's ability to pursue a post-secondary education depends heavily on the province in which he or she lives, and the province in which he or she wishes to study.

This is a direct result of the differing levels of commitment on the part of provincial governments to making higher education accessible, available and affordable. Most ironically, the so-called 'have' provinces have often demonstrated less of a commitment to PSE and have therefore ranked lower on our scale of comparison than many of the so-called 'have-not' provinces. Legislative and fiscal choices imposed by provincial leaders are as significant as a lack of federal funds.

Although the analysis of higher education is generally quite limited in the mainstream media, there are many researchers, activists and authors who are constantly investigating the changes taking place in post-secondary education, and with what effect. Furthermore, Statistics Canada does provide vital research in this domain, on which we have relied heavily in determining where government fiscal policies vis-à-vis education are situated.

As with previous editions of *Missing Pieces*, we are pleased to provide readers with articles and essays that deal with a wide variety of important issues relating to the state of higher education in Canada. Each article shows the degree to which equity, quality, accessibility/opportunity/affordability, and public accountability are implicated in the restructuring of post-secondary education. They focus on issues inadequately examined—or not discussed at all—in the mainstream media, and how students, faculty, support staff, and researchers at the university and college level are affected by government policies. They also explain how events and policies taking place on university and college campuses and in boardrooms across the country have profound implications for all Canadians.

Once again, *Missing Pieces* provides an overview of higher education in each province to indicate changes that may have taken place in the previous year, as well as proposed government initiatives that may alter the course of higher education in the future.

How do we speak of higher education in Canada? What is the link between education and training? How do notions of capital and investment intersect with education and social development? These and other questions are discussed in Bob Baldwin's paper, "Access to education and training," and John McMurtry's "Education and human capital."

University finance in Canada has undergone a series of changes, often reflecting the priorities of provincial governments, but also of university administrations. Where has funding been allocated? How have faculty fared? To what extent has private money become a factor in sponsored research? Can any implications be drawn as to the new "priorities" for higher learning in Canada? Ron Melchers provides an overview of major changes to university finance since the release of the previous edition of *Missing Pieces*.

How have the policies of universities and colleges in a cost-cutting climate been experienced by faculty and support staff? How is the quality of the learning and teaching environment affected? Are we witnessing the creation of an academic underclass? Vicky Smallman examines the situation in which sessional instructors find themselves on campuses across the country in "Resisting casualization: contract academic staff mobilize."

In "The university as a workplace in the global context," Theresa Healy discusses the impact of various aspects of education restructuring, global trade deals and privatization on support staff at Ontario universities.

How has academic freedom fared, particularly given recent political events that have increased the distrust and surveillance of political discourse, or in some cases any criticism of academic and political administration whatsoever? What are the implications of this control—not just on faculty, but on the quality of education these institutions of higher learning offer? How does this further an already-entrenched agenda of corporatization? David Noble, author of *Digital Diploma Mills: The automation of higher education*, tackles some of these questions, particularly since the events of September 11.

The cases of Nancy Olivieri, David Healy and David Noble have received a certain amount of coverage in the national and international press, and have succeeded in raising some of the questions about corporatization on campus, limits on academic freedom, and public accountability. However, the corporate presence on campus and in academic research is still profound. Lucy Sharratt discusses the growing influence of biotechnology and corporate funding of Canadian research in "Big biotech bucks buys the building."

As universities and colleges are encouraged—even required—to become more "innovative" and entrepreneurial, is the relationship between the institution, its faculty, and the broader public altered? Does this have any effect on the funding of research and on research directions? Does a philosophy of inter-institutional competition change the role of institutions of higher learning? To what extent is the business community involved in this shift? Claire Polster examines these and other issues in "University competition: New trouble in the making."

How have the many changes or priorities reflected in institutions of higher learning affected the quality of education those institutions are capable of delivering? In other words, how do we determine or define a "high-quality" education? Of course, these questions—as with the category of "quality"—are necessarily broad; we have maintained throughout these three editions of *Missing Pieces* that quality is not merely the sum total of so-called measurable outcomes. How do we ensure that institutions—and the faculty and staff, as well as students within them—are capable of contributing to, receiving, and making use of a high-quality education and a high-quality learning environment? Michael Temelini addresses a number of these issues in "What is a high-quality education?" In "Dumbing down distance education: The corporate agenda and the end of quality," Jennifer Sumner examines the degree to which distance learning, largely because of its corporate-determined priorities, has profound and disturbing implications for quality education.

The issue of access and affordability are fundamental in discussions about higher education in Canada. Student debt, an issue of growing concern, especially since 1993, has received some attention in the mainstream media as debt loads grow and as an increasing number of low-income students find it difficult or impossible to pursue PSE. A number of provincial governments have instituted tuition fee freezes or rollbacks, but other provinces have continued to allow higher education to become priced out of range for many students. Other universities have lobbied for outright tuition fee deregulation, while some specialty programs have already been deregulated and their price tags adjusted accordingly.

As the federal and provincial governments come under public pressure to address the issue of student debt, several reports have been released that examine this issue. One paper, published in the C.D. Howe Institute's *Commentary*, by Ross Finnie (November 2001), examines student debt loads in Canada, with the stated goal of "easing the burden." Finnie, however, appears to advocate higher tuition fees (and therefore expanded debt levels) to compensate for declining levels of government support. In "Increasing the burden: Student financial assistance in Canada," Mike Conlon and Pam Frache of the Canadian Federation of Students confront Finnie's arguments and examine the critical situation of student debt in Canada.

This is by no means a complete picture of the state of higher education in Canada. Once again, we as editors encourage readers to take the content of all editions of *Missing Pieces* into consideration when attempting to analyze many of the changes taking place on university and college campuses, and the implications of those changes for all Canadians. But the discussion needs to go much further. There is a marked lack of information available to the public about the true state of student debt, and how tuition fee deregulation and other higher education funding policies affect various income groups, in ways ranging from minimal to devastating.

There needs to be much greater attention paid to the degree of corporate involvement on campuses and in university research. Whose needs are being served? Who is being silenced? Who is suffering? What does this mean for education quality, or the public good? These questions are particularly significant in light of recent limitations placed on academic freedom, and have everything to do with fundamentally changing the relationship between educational institutions and the public—and their responsibilities to each other.

How do these changes—competitiveness between institutions, cost-cutting measures, tuition fee deregulation, targeted funding, the prevalence of distance learning and IT—change our expectations of higher education, or our relationship to it? What are the implications for the quality of education these institutions are able to provide? How is the public—the entire public—being served?

The Trent Central Student Association at Trent University has taken the indicators used in this and in previous editions of *Missing Pieces* to conduct their own school audit and document how their university has responded to government policies and priorities. It provides a much more detailed picture that those offered in conventional school rankings, and should be compulsory reading for any student interested in attending that institution. We encourage other student or faculty groups to undertake their own audits to provide a more thorough and accurate description of the education offered at their institution. Who sits on the board of governors? Which corporations are represented? How many food banks are on campus? What are average tuition fees for domestic and international students? Which corporations have a presence on campus or in university or college research? What is the student/faculty ratio? How is funding being spent? What success stories should the public know about? These are some of the factors of which prospective students need to be aware before considering a particular university or college—and which would greatly inform the Canadian public as to the state of higher education at each post-secondary institution in the country. It would be far more appropriate—and useful—than comparing fundraising results between the University of Toronto and Trent University, for example.

We express our appreciation for those students, researchers, organizations and faculty who contributed their time, advice and expertise to broadening and enriching the discussions surrounding higher education in Canada. And, once again, we look forward to continuing these discussions to ensure that higher education will be of the highest possible quality—equitable, affordable, and accessible to all, and accountable to the public it serves.❖

Endnotes

1   Details may be found at http://www.policyalternatives.ca.

Provincial rankings

Missing Pieces III documents some interesting changes from previous editions of this report. However, there are some significant consistencies: once again, Ontario ranks last in its commitment to PSE, falling even further behind in equity and remaining dead last in accountability and quality.

This year Quebec and B.C. switched positions. Considering the political direction of the new B.C. government, this decline can be seen as a premonition of things to come. In fact, B.C. is already showing a decline in equity and quality, improving only in accessibility—which is already in the process of being reversed, although that is not reflected in this current set of statistics.

Notable are Newfoundland's improvement (from 7th to 4th), and Nova Scotia's and New Brunswick's decline (from 4th to 6th and 6th to 9th, respectively). Newfoundland has implemented a tuition fee freeze and rollback, and improved its commitment to equity (though this was largely because of the declining commitment to equity on the part of other provinces). On the other hand, Nova Scotia's tuition fees throw PSE accessibility into jeopardy and contribute to this province's poorer showing.

New Brunswick's sharply declining commitment to quality contributed to its poor overall ranking. Saskatchewan also demonstrated a slight improvement, specifically in the area of quality, which accounts for its improved ranking.

Overall rankings

Province	Equity Rank	Quality Rank	Accountability Ranking	Accessibility Ranking	Overall MP3 Rank	Overall MP2 Rank
NF	10	2	3	4	4	7
PEI	9	3	4	5	5	6
NS	1	7	9	7	6	4
NB	6	9	8	8	9	6
PQ	4	1	1	1	1	2
ON	7	10	10	6	10	10
MB	3	3	5	4	3	3
SK	8	5	7	9	7	9
AB	6	7	7	10	8	8
BC	3	6	2	2	2	1

Equity

Equity is defined as those mechanisms in place at a provincial level to ensure that all students, regardless of gender, place of origin, or socioeconomic status, can make optimal use of higher education in whichever location and discipline they choose. It also requires that those opportunities not only be protected, but also reinforced and thoroughly integrated into every aspect of higher education. It also refers to the facilitation of full participation in the higher education experience by all members of the post-secondary community—students as well as faculty, support staff, and administration.

Equity

Province	% Change International Student Participation	% of International University Students	Women as a % of Tenured Faculty	Unemployment Rate	Inequality Index	Equity Rank	MP2 Equity Rank
NF	5	10	8	10	10	10	10
PEI	2	9	4	9	9	9	9
NS	3	3	1	7	4	1	3
NB	1	7	2	8	8	6	7
PQ	7	1	5	6	6	4	5
ON	6	8	6	4	3	7	6
MB	10	4	3	2	5	3	2
SK	4	6	9	3	7	8	8
AB	8	5	10	1	2	6	4
BC	9	2	7	5	1	3	1

Provincial commitment to equity in PSE

Provincial governments demonstrate varying degrees of commitment to the principle of equity: for example, Newfoundland performs poorly in its percentage of international students, the unemployment rate, and the inequality index (% of population with less than secondary education compared to the % of population with PSE). But Newfoundland bettered its ranking in the percentage of women on its tenured faculty.

Nova Scotia demonstrates the greatest commitment to maintaining equity in PSE, moving from 3rd to 1st overall: for the second year in a row it scores 1st in women as a percentage of tenured faculty, 3rd in the percentage of international students, and 4th in the inequality index.

Both Alberta and B.C. reduced their commitment to equity (from 4th to 6th and 1st to 3rd, respectively). Both provinces reduced their percentage of women as tenured faculty.

Accessibility, affordability and opportunity

We have defined accessibility (including affordability and opportunity) as the freedom to obtain and make use of a post-secondary education. It provides an examination of the financial measures in place to ensure that students are able to afford to attend the university or college of their choice, to complete their education, and to have the opportunity to use that education upon graduation.

The accessibility ranking is determined largely by how the provinces have participated in eliminating—or at least mitigating—financial barriers to university and college.

Accessibility, affordability and opportunity

Province	Average Undergrad University Fees	Average College Tuition Fees	% Yr-to-Yr Change in University Fees	% Yr-to-Yr Change in College Fees	Percentage Change in University Tuition Fees	Percentage Change in College Tuition Fees	PSE Participation Rate (18-24 yrs)	Accessibility Ranking	MP2 Accessibility Ranking
NF	4	4	1	6	6	7	4	4	7
PEI	5	7	8	6	4	3	5	5	5
NS	10	6	7	10	8	6	2	7	3
NB	6	8	9	6	5	10	6	8	8
PQ	1	1	4	6	2	1	1	1	1
ON	9	5	5	7	9	5	3	6	7
MB	3	3	3	6	3	4	10	4	3
SK	7	9	10	8	7	8	8	9	9
AB	8	10	6	9	10	9	7	10	10
BC	2	2	2	1	1	2	9	2	4

Provincial commitment to accessibility, affordability and opportunity in PSE

Newfoundland improved its commitment to accessibility this year from 7th to 4th, due largely to a rollback in university tuition fees and a freeze in college tuition fees (for both college and university tuition fees, Newfoundland ranks 4th in the country).

While B.C.'s ranking improved from 4th to 2nd, it should be noted that this was due to a rollback in tuition fees. The new provincial government has just reversed this policy, ensuring that next year's results for B.C. will be much less impressive.

Less positively, Nova Scotia slipped from 3rd to 7th in accessibility, due largely to high university tuition fees and its high percentage change in university and college tuition fees over the past decade.

Missing Pieces III

Quality

We have defined quality as the degree of excellence of the entire educational experience. A high quality education depends on the provincial and federal governments' commitment to fostering a well-rounded educational experience and environment. In part, this includes: the quality of student life; the adequacy of university or college finances; the breadth of disciplines and modes of learning offered; and student access to tenured faculty.

Quality

Province	% Change in Fulltime Faculty	University Student/ Faculty Ratio	Per Capita Provincial Expenditure on PSE	% Change in Per Capita Expenditure	Provincial University Operating Grants per Capita	% Change Provincial University Operating Grants	Quality Rank	MP2 Quality Rank
NF	6	3	5	4	2	4	2	6
PEI	1	1	10	6	7	2	3	5
NS	3	4	8	8	5	10	7	8
NB	10	6	6	7	4	9	9	1
PQ	8	7	1	5	1	1	1	3
ON	5	10	9	10	10	5	10	10
MB	9	2	3	1	4	8	3	5
SK	4	8	2	3	6	7	5	9
AB	2	9	4	9	8	6	7	8
BC	7	5	7	2	9	3	6	2

Provincial commitment to quality in PSE

Once again, Ontario demonstrates the lowest commitment to quality in PSE, due to the highest student/faculty ratio in the country, the greatest reduction in provincial expenditures on PSE, and the lowest provincial operating grants per-capita.

Quebec improved its rank from 3rd to 1st this year, due in part to its increase in provincial university operating grants, which are the highest in the country (up from 5th).

Manitoba improved its rank from 5th to 3rd, largely because of its per-capita expenditure on PSE and the percentage change in expenditure from last year.

Saskatchewan also improved from 9th to 5th, having increased its per-capita provincial expenditure on PSE and improving its rank in percentage change of full-time faculty (although it should be noted that Saskatchewan still has one of the higher student/faculty ratios in the country).

Newfoundland also improved its placing from 6th to 2nd, due in part to its (comparatively speaking) high levels of university operating grants and its improvement in percentage change in full-time faculty.

Public accountability

Accountability is defined as the degree to which provincial governments ensure that universities and colleges are in fact accountable to the public, and not to corporations or individual sponsors or clients. In addition, it means that universities and colleges, and their functions of teaching, research and community service, remain in the public domain and are not privatized. This is determined largely by the amount of public funding dedicated to post-secondary education budgets, as compared to funding from private donations or student fees, which download the cost of education to individuals.

Accountability

Province	% of Total PSE Budget Received from Student Fees	% of Total PSE Budget Received from Gov't Grants	% of Total PSE Budget Received from Private Sources	After High School 18-20 year old PSE Continuers	Educational attainment	Needs-based ranking	Accountability Ranking	MP2 Accountability Ranking
NF	6	2	2	3	9	4	3	3
PEI	7	7	1	4	7	6	4	5
NS	10	10	6	2	2	10	9	9
NB	8	8	3	6	8	6	8	8
PQ	1	1	9	1	5	2	1	2
ON	9	9	10	7	4	9	10	10
MB	5	3	8	9	6	4	5	5
SK	2	4	5	8	10	8	7	6
AB	4	7	7	10	1	8	7	8
BC	3	5	4	5	3	1	2	1

Provincial commitment to public accountability

There were some changes in provincial commitment to public accountability, although Quebec remained in first place and Ontario in last. This is consistent with the degree to which provincial governments have taken responsibility for the education of their students; the degree to which they have (or have not) downloaded the financial burden onto individuals or their families; and the degree to which PSE relies on private funding sources, (potentially jeopardizing the degree to which PSE is accountable to the public as opposed to private funders).

This category also indicates the degree to which governments have demonstrated accountability to those students who take longer to complete their degree, because governments are responsible to all citizens at all stages of their education.

Newfoundland & Labrador

Staff research

The province's public post-secondary institutions consist of Memorial University of Newfoundland and the College of the North Atlantic. Memorial University is made up of the St. John's campus and the Fisheries and Marine Institute located in St. John's; and the Sir Wilfred Grenfell College located in Corner Brook. Matters of an academic character are in the general charge of the Senate of the University.

The University has six faculties and seven schools offering degrees at various levels. Certificate and Diploma programs are available in selected areas as well. The College of the North Atlantic is governed by a provincial board and administered by a single executive office.

There are 18 college campuses across the province offering over 70 full-time programs and more than 300 part-time courses.

Budget decisions

In 1994, the Government of Newfoundland and Labrador eliminated the provincial needs-based non-repayable study grants program, replacing it with a student loan program. The grant program had been available to university and college students since 1978. The Newfoundland Student Loans Remission Program was instituted, yet it fell far from its original mandate. That year the average student loans increased by approximately 100% for university students, 75% for public college students, and 170% for private college students. The total value of loans borrowed by students increased from $36 million in 1993 to over $160 million in 1997.

The 2002-2003 budget will likely not contain any major government funding for the upcoming university budget. The Newfoundland government pays the majority of Memorial's operating costs. Last year, the province contributed $150 million of MUN's quarter-billion dollar budget, with 27% of its revenue coming from tuition fees. The remainder of the budget came through other financial sources.

Memorial has millions of dollars in infrastructure maintenance costs which require immediate attention. The university is also coming under criticism for expanding its engineering and applied science operations at the expense of arts and music.

About $4 million was allocated for the creation of the Student Investment and Opportunities Corporation to establish work programs for young people, targeting rural areas where there aren't as many job opportunities.

Tuition fees

The province announced in the 1999 budget a two-year tuition freeze, which was then extended to the 2001-2002 academic year for both the University and the College of the North Atlantic. Also included in that budget was a $10-million increase to the student loans program to deal with the costs incurred since the banks ended their participation in the loans program. The 2000 provincial budget also saw the creation of the Labour Market Development Council, an advisory council to look into the post-secondary education system to see if it responds to the changing economy.

The 2001 budget contained a 10% cut in tuition fees for students, effective September 2001. The cut applied to undergraduates at Memorial, but not to international students, medical students, or students at the College of the North Atlantic.

Premier Roger Grimes often cites his government's emphasis on youth policies. "The likelihood is that we'll have many hundreds of more post-secondary students in Newfoundland and Labrador who'll have an opportunity for employment in all regions," he said. The Premier has indicated an intention to continue with measures to reduce student debt in future years.

However, the tuition fee debate has taken a rather bizare twist in this province. Premier Grimes has proposed allowing bulk water exports, which had been banned by the legislature in 1999, as compensation for the price of free tuition. The Premier said that Newfoundland's fresh water supplies would not be negatively impacted, but that the estimated $70 million revenue would be enough to ensure that all Newfoundland students have access to free tuition. Students have stated that they refuse to have their concerns pitted against environmental ones.

Student aid

Student groups in the province have called for a system of non-repayable grants to all students and a means of compensation for all required educational and learning materials. They have also advocated increasing the minimum wage to a living wage.

Students have also raised the issue of revamping the current student loan system. Edulinx, owned by CIBC, is the company that handles student loans. Students point out that Edulinx is turning the student loan system into a for-profit business, which exacerbates the issue of high debt loads for students.

The Department of Education is looking into the possibility of changing the status of a full-time student to four courses per semester, up from three. Students who are single parents, students with disabilities, and lower-income students more commonly take partial course loads and will therefore be more negatively affected by these proposed changes because part-time students receive less from student aid than full-time students. If the amendment is implemented, students who are most in need of student aid will not qualify for a full student loan.

A joint initiative between the Association of Atlantic Universities (AAU) and the Atlantic Provinces Economic Council (APEC), *Our Universities: The Key to Atlantic Canada's Future* is calling for increased funding from the public sector towards the region's universities. This report stated that a university education provides greater access to full-time rather than part-time employment, and that the universities are one of Atlantic Canada's greatest resources. The report examines the economic impact of students on the region's economy, the relation between a university education and the unemployment rate, and the growing enrolment in Atlantic Canada's universities.

While the necessity for more people to obtain a higher education has been growing, the report maintains that funding from both the provincial and federal government have been inadequate to meet this growing need.

International students

Memorial is actively recruiting international students from all parts of the world, because they pay higher tuition fees and bring in thousands of dollars a year to the provincial economy through living expenses. But the President of Memorial maintains that Newfoundland students benefit greatly from exposure to people from other cultures, and denies that the university is pursuing foreign students for the purpose of generating revenue.

Faculty

The Canadian Association of University Teachers is hosting a series of discussions on various issues affecting post-secondary education as part of a cross-Canada series of hearings. The consensus of the hearings held in Newfoundland was that this province is facing serious problems due to public policy decisions by both levels of government.

Newfoundland used to have free tuition several decades ago, but now students are paying much more, and receiving far less.

Memorial has been losing professors for the last decade. The History Department will be losing five professors at the end of this year, while the Geography Department has seen its numbers cut almost in half since the mid-90s. Faculty that are retiring or lost to other schools have not been replaced.

In response, departments have reduced the number of elective courses offered, and increased class size for the first-year courses, limiting student access to faculty. Departments now have to compete with one another to maintain or increase their faculty numbers.

Faculty members are concerned with how a greatly reduced staff will jeopardize their attempt to maintain program integrity. Yet Vice-President Academic Evan Simpson cites *Maclean's* magazine's ranking of Memorial, placing it near the top of Canadian universities in terms of favourable student-teacher ratios as evidence that there is no need to increase the number of faculty.

However, teaching staff at the university has dropped by a quarter in the past decade, and students are bearing the brunt of these cuts. The university is moving away from hiring tenure-track faculty and hiring more non-tenured teaching staff. Low pay, inadequate office space, and uncertain contract renewals are leading to low morale among non-tenured staff, making the university less attractive to potential professors. ❖

Prince Edward Island
Staff research

Holland College and the University of Prince Edward Island are the public higher education institutions on P.E.I. Holland College offers diverse technical and vocational programmes leading to a Certificate or Diploma. UPEI offers mainly undergraduate degrees, and houses the regional Atlantic Veterinary College, which provides undergraduate and graduate education in Veterinary Medicine.

In 1999, UPEI was granted the authority to offer graduate level degrees. Masters programs are offered in Education in Leadership and Learning, Science in Biology and Chemistry. In addition, UPEI offers a Master of Science program and a doctoral-level in Veterinary Medicine through the Atlantic Veterinary College. The College serves all of the Atlantic provinces.

French post-secondary education programs are delivered through la Société Educative de l'Ile-du-Prince Edouard and the Collège de l'Acadie, a satellite office of the Nova Scotia Collège de l'Acadie. There are 20 private vocational or career training colleges that registered with the Department of Education.

Provincial funding

Over the last number of years, the provincial government has been providing increases in the University of Prince Edward Island operating grant in the amounts of $1.2 million in 2000/2001, an additional million in 2001/2002, and a further million dollars for 2002/2003. This will bring the UPEI operating grant up to $18.5 million.

UPEI's undergraduate tuition levels are the third lowest in the Maritime region. Tuition fees for Canadian students were $3,480 and $6,880 for international students. Only St. Thomas University and the Université de Moncton have lower fees in the Atlantic region. UPEI did not increase fees on the main campus in 2001.

The undergraduate Arts and Science students' tuition fees for this year are $3,690. That compares to the average in New Brunswick with $3,838 and an average tuition fee in Nova Scotia of $4,908. While tuition fees at Holland College are $2,000, there is a mandatory "technology fee" of approximately $1,200—this ensures that Holland college's fees are among the highest in the country—to compensate for inadequate provincial funding of the college system. Furthermore, tuition fees in Prince Edward Island are not regulated by the provincial government: they are determined by the individual institutions.

In the year 2000, the Island Student Awards Program was introduced. University students in their third and forth year of study receive $600 each year, and to date almost 1,200 Island students have received awards under this program. The government has not made any promise to freeze tuition fees for the coming year, despite a request from students. But the Premier has stated in the legislature: "I want to assure students that we will continue to work with UPEI to try to keep tuition fees as competitive as possible."

The Community Service Bursary Program was also introduced in 2000, with a maximum award of $500. Since the program began in April 2000, more than 600 students have participated. More than 200 community organizations have signed on with the program and help provide students with an opportunity to participate. In addition, there is a Debt Reduction Program, which provides grants upon graduation of up to $2,000 per year of study and if their student loan is $6,000 or more in a year of study. The Interest Relief Program provides relief for up to five years, in terms of the interest on their student loans.

The government signed an agreement with the Island Credit Unions in November 2001, allowing students receiving provincial student loans to be served by one of 13 Island credit unions. This agreement will remain in effect until July 2006. Island credit unions have become the exclusive lender for the provincial student loan program.

In response to the health care crisis, the government is expanding the number of nurses in the province, with the creation of 14 new seats at the UPEI School of Nursing. The expansion will bring the total number of seats to 59, an increase of 31%. In four years there will be a total of 56 additional places at the UPEI School of Nursing.

A new Student Centre is being build with money raised by the students with support from the university and $1 million from the government.

In 1994/95, the revenue received from the Canada Health and Social Transfer (CHST) was about $91 million, (11% of provincial revenues). Today, funding through CHST is only $88 million without factoring in the effect of inflation. Federal transfers are not keeping up to the demands of health or education. But the federal government did lift the cap on the on Equalization payments for one year, and that has helped since the Island economy is now growing.

UPEI joins ranks of unionized faculty

The University of Prince Edward Island Faculty Association successfully concluded its unionization drive with the August 2 certification order of the P.E.I. Labour Relations Board. Whereas the faculty association had previously represented only full-time teachers, it will now bargain for all academic staff engaged in teaching in a university degree course and/or engaged in research, as well as all librarians.

The P.E.I. Labour Relations Board determined the union had such majority support in the membership cards submitted that no representation vote was required. Under P.E.I. law, the Labour Board has discretionary authority to order a vote." Eighty per cent of the faculties of Canada's university are currently unionized, and St. Francis Xavier University is the only other university in Atlantic Canada where the faculty is not unionized.

Research

Last January, three researchers (out of a pool of 208 projects across the country) at UPEI received $3.6 million in new funding from Canada Foundation for Innovation.

Professor Cathy Chan and colleagues received $2,004,905 to develop an Atlantic Centre for Comparative Biomedical Research.

The UPEI Office of Research Development and the Department of Computer Services received $165,514 for a network upgrade to enable high-speed access to research resources.

Dr. Annabel Cohen, a professor of psychology, was awarded $1,492,272 for an Institute for Interdisciplinary Research in Culture, Multimedia, Technology and Cognition.❖

Nova Scotia overview
By Theresa C. Sabourin

In March 2001, a draft policy document from the Government of Nova Scotia was leaked. The policy outlined plans to tie funding for post-secondary education institutions to default rates for student loans. Two days later, Minister of Finance Neil LeBlanc released the 2001-2002 provincial budget, which outlined a vision for post-secondary funding that would focus on providing students with basic job skills. The government's proposed de-designation policy will play an important role in changing the way colleges and universities in Nova Scotia are funded to reflect this new direction.

Rather than providing students with the broad range of skills and knowledge needed in today's rapidly changing economy, this policy will compel universities and colleges to design curriculum to respond to the transitory and often unpredictable trends in the job market. The direction that has been articulated is one in which post-secondary funding will become increasingly tied to short-term labour market trends.

A government-induced crisis

In the last decade, tuition fees in Nova Scotia have increased by 115%, making Nova Scotia's tuition fees the highest in the country. Fees rose by 4.9% in 2001-2002, bringing average tuition fees to $4,732 per year. Nova Scotia also has the lowest government contributions to university operating budgets as a percentage, at 43.4% in 1999-2000. In addition, the provincial government has eliminated all non-repayable student financial assistance over the past decade.

In 1994, the government eliminated its student bursary program, and in 2000 the loan remission program was wiped out. The Nova Scotia government has also chosen to re-direct federal funds from the Millennium Scholarship Foundation into general revenues. The government is in essence withholding federal funds that were earmarked to help alleviate student debt.

While the cost of a post-secondary education has been increasing for individual students, and while government expenditures on non-repayable financial assistance have been phased out, the cost to government for servicing student loans has increased. Since the banks pulled out of student loans in 2000, the N.S. government has signed several short-term extensions with the Royal Bank to continue administering provincial student loans. While the agreements have not been made public, it is apparent that the government is paying premiums of over $3 million per year, even though the Royal Bank no longer accepts any of the risks associated with collection of the loans. This amounts to an administration fee of over 10% on a total yearly student loan portfolio of approximately $30 million.

In addition, the cost to government for providing interest relief has more than doubled since 1998-99. Government spending on interest relief increased to over $3.5 million in 2000-2001 from $1.7 million in 1998-99. Much of this increase can be attributed to costs associated with the increasing difficulty students face in managing ever-increasing debt loads. As student debt levels rise, a growing number of students are forced to access the interest relief program. As funding is removed from grant and loan remission programs, more funding is required to cover interest costs on the increased principal. This increase is essentially a transfer of government funding from dollars spent on reducing actual debt levels to dollars paid to banks to cover interest costs on larger debts.

A misdirected response

The N.S. government is currently putting the final touches on a policy that will see student loan eligibility and program funding tied to student loan default rates. Designation is the process by which post-secondary institutions are deemed eligible for student loans. Currently all public universities and colleges in Nova Scotia are designated, and students attending those institutions are able to apply for provincial and federal government loans. Under the proposed policy, a program that has higher than acceptable student loan default rates would be de-designated or the college or university in question would bear the cost of student loan defaults. Students who are enrolled in these programs would likely no longer be eligible for government student loans.

Tying student loan default rates to designation of programs for student loan eligibility is in part an effort to reduce government expenditures on student loans by limiting the ability of students to access them. Rather than addressing high debt-loads by re-introducing grants and reducing tuition fees, the government will be able to reduce student debt by making many students ineligible to receive loans in the first place.

At the same time, the policy will provide a tool for government to reduce funding for many programs. Enrolment in de-designated programs would be affected as students on government loans would no longer be eligible and/or the program could directly lose a portion of its funding from government as institutions are forced to cover the costs of the defaults.

This policy will negatively impact institutions in economically depressed parts of the province. Institutions which serve students from the local community in areas with high unemployment rates could be at particularly high risk for de-designation. If enough programs are de-designated at one institution, the college or university in question could essentially become de-designated. At institutions such as the University College of Cape Breton, where over 50% of all students are forced to access student loans, a policy of de-designation could cut the university's enrolment by half overnight.

A narrowing focus

For the past decade, government underfunding has increasingly limited access to post-secondary education for lower- and middle-income Nova Scotians. The Nova Scotia government's new direction will further limit accessibility to a college or university education, and undermine the very idea of the Nova Scotia student assistance program.

These policies will promote a system of post-secondary education that is subject to the whims of the notoriously unreliable labour market. Universities and colleges will be forced to design curriculum motivated only by the threat of de-designation. Rather than producing graduates with an education that will allow them to adapt to changing circumstances, short-term outcomes will be given priority. These policies will systematically dismantle the public post-secondary system to the extent that it does not meet the government's narrowing focus.❖

Sources

Budget Address: Province of Nova Scotia for the Fiscal Year 2001-02 presented to the Nova Scotia House of Assembly by the Honourable Neil J. LeBlanc, March 29, 2001.

Nova Scotia House of Assembly Hansard, March 28, 2001, p.296-298.

Government of Nova Scotia, *Draft Nova Scotia Student Assistance Policy for Designation of Educational Institutions for Student Loan Purposes*, November 2000.

Dennis Cochrane, Nova Scotia Deputy Minister of Education, Letter to the University of King's College Students' Union, November 26, 2001.

Statistics Canada, *The Daily*, August 27, 2001.

Statistics Canada, *The Daily*, July 30, 2001.

New Brunswick
Staff research

Private school – public funds

On June 11, 2001, after the province of New Brunswick received 'guidance' from KPMG, a for-profit consulting firm, the provincial government granted Lansbridge Universtiy the ability to award Master's Degrees.

But there is strong public opposition to the provincial government's accreditation of Lansbridge, a wholly Internet-based company owned by Learnsoft Corporation of Ottawa. Lansbridge originally opened as Unexus University in Fredericton in 1999, and has received $375,000 from the Atlantic Canada Opportunities Agency and $225,000 from Human Resources Development Canada.

At a time when governments bemoan a lack of dollars to use for higher education and amidst the failure of ITI, any public education funds for a private for-profit is questionable public policy. Lansbridge and DeVry Institute of Technology (Alberta and Ontario) are Canada's officially recognized for-profit universities.

The Canadian Association of University Teachers (CAUT) is concerned about the implications Lansbridge will have with regard to Canada's international trade obligations. "Public services like education are generally protected from trade agreements as long as they are provided by governments, on a not-for-profit basis, and not in competition with other providers," said Tom Booth, president of CAUT. "Given that Lansbridge is a for-profit enterprise, we are worried that its accreditation could expose post-secondary education to the disciplines of trade agreements."

Faculty: employment equity

The number of full-time faculty in New Brunswick declined between 1990 and 1998 by 10%, while enrolment remained relatively static. In 1991, a review of employment equity in New Brunswick's universities concluded that an increase in the number of women with Ph.D.s would be reflected in future hirings for academic positions. By 1999, some progress had been made, but a representative work force has still not been realized.

The percentage of female faculty and librarians in New Brunswick universities runs from a low of 27% at UNB at Fredericton to a high of 50% at

Shippagan. In 1988, the percentage of female faculty range at all the universitites ran from 13% to 47%.

Retention

Members of the Association of University of New Brunswick Teachers, with members in Fredericton, Saint John, Bathurst and Moncton, ratified a new four-year collective agreement, retroactive to July 1, 2001. This contract will help maintain UNB's high-quality education and research status by ensuring competitive salaries and comparable workloads. However, in order to deal with a wave of retirements expected over the decade, more must be done to improve research funding in the province.

Between 1989 and 1998, the entire amount spent on research and development in New Brunswick fell from a high of $163 million to only $126 million, a decline of more than 20%. On a per capita basis, this represents only one-third of the average amount of funding that the other provinces are spending on research.

In New Brunswick, there are few commercial enterprises with research facilities; therefore, the majority of R&D is done at the public universities. The innovative capacity of the public institutions is hindered by a lack of equipment, infrastructure and operating dollars caused by the absence of meaningful levels of government research funding over the last decade.

Funding and student aid

Premier Bernard Lord has demonstrated his commitment to higher education by responding to the Working Group on Accessibility to Post-Secondary Education in New Brunswick, with an injection of an additional $5.1 million in bursaries to be allocated over the next three years. This addition will help develop a vibrant labour market.

Post-secondary education remains an important component of economic growth and stability in New Brunswick. In 2000, the unemployment rate of university graduates sat at 4.4%, while those with only a high school education were unemployed at a rate of 10.5%.

Unfortunately, any additional funds used for student grants may be eaten up by continued increases in tuition fees. Over the last decade, university fees have increased by nearly 90%, with a 7.4% jump from 2000 to 2001 alone bringing undergraduate fees to $3,779. College tuition fees in 1999–00 were the highest in the country at an average of $2,400. Having recognized this, the provincial government has frozen college fees at this level for the past two years.

The total revenue collected from student fees for the 2000-01 school year was $77.3 million, up from $50.4 for 1992-93. Student fees account for 23% of all revenues for universities in the province—the second highest percentage in the country.

Federal transfer funds for New Brunswick higher education fell from $17.4 million in 1992 to $14.4 in 2000, while revenue from the provincial government rose from $146 million to $151.7 million.❖

Performing for the market in Quebec
By David Bernans

Thanks to a strong student movement in Quebec, the provincial government has not been able to download the cost of post-secondary education onto the backs of students to the same extent as other provinces. In 1995-96, after a wave of strikes and occupations, students won a provincial tuition freeze. Thus, even during the period of budget cuts, from 1994-1998, Quebec managed to maintain levels of public financing higher than most other provinces and to keep tuition levels well below the Canadian average. Even out-of-province university students, who now pay an extra $68 per credit (which can add up to $2,040 per year), are still paying less than they would if they were studying in Ontario.

Nevertheless, the budget cuts (over $300 million was cut in annual funding to universities between 1994 and 1998) were felt in the form of larger class sizes, reduction of faculty, fewer programs, and new "user fees" (read backdoor tuition increases). In February of 2000, when Education Minister François Legault (a former CEO of Air Transat) announced that a "reinvestment" of $1 billion would be injected into the province's universities and Cégeps and youth programs over the next three years, students, staff and faculty breathed a collective sigh of relief.

As a glance at the 2000/01 figures for "University and College Revenue through transfers from provincial governments" will show, Quebec's funding compares favourably with those of other provinces. The new billion-dollar promise has not even started to kick in, yet Quebec surpasses the economic powerhouse of Ontario in total provincial transfers (about $3 billion vs about $2.8 billion, respectively).

All that glitters, however, is not gold. The new money that is being injected this year has considerable strings attached. Following in the footsteps of a growing number of U.S. states and heeding the recommendations of international financial institutions like the World Bank, Legault used this opportunity to introduce "performance-based funding." All the new university funding will be conditional on meeting certain "performance" criteria. Performance would be assured through "performance contracts" negotiated between the Ministry of Education (MEQ) and each university. Following a similar model, Cégeps would be forced to adopt "success plans" [plans de réussite]. And who, after all, could be against performance or success?

Of course, everything depends on what criteria are used to judge performance or success. In the case of university funding, the performance of each university is judged on a series of "performance indicators." Before performance is tied to funding, it is often measured on a variety of indicators, including enrolments or graduation rates by ethnicity or by gender. Once performance is tied to funding, however, the market model tends to predominate. Under our new funding scheme in Quebec, "performance" is a synonym for market-defined "efficiency."

Following the directives of the MEQ, Quebec's universities drafted performance contracts over the course of the 2000-01 academic year. Each contract would set targets on a variety of performance indicators for years to come. Presumably, failure to draft a contract acceptable to the MEQ would have resulted in a loss of funding equivalent to the institution's share of the $600 million reinvestment. Since all universities chose to follow the MEQ directives, we will never know if the ministry was bluffing. Every Quebec university has now locked itself into performance targets, and failure to achieve those targets could result in a loss of funding. Furthermore, the new performance data create a basis for comparison not only between Quebec's universities, but also between all universities around the world that adopt the World Bank's recommended performance criteria. This is globalization's "race to the bottom" in the public education sector.

By agreeing to the performance targets, universities are committing to specific goals on the following:

- attracting corporate funding (more research for private interests and less for the public interest), increasing "efficient use of human resources" (reducing labour costs);
- rationalization of program offerings (cutting programs that are not "competitive");
- increasing teaching loads (reducing time for independent research and advising); and
- increasing degree completion and reducing time to completion rates (weeding out low income students, students with part-time jobs, and other "high risk" groups).

The MEQ effectively makes it impossible to increase degree completion and reduce time to completion rates through more generous student aid packages because universities must also agree to stop running deficits. No performance targets have been set for accessibility. No targets have been set for quality of education (unless one considers the ability to attract corporate funding or the "competitivity" of a program to be an accurate measure of quality). No targets have been set for equity, whether it be in terms of enrolments by gender or ethnicity, or in terms of reducing faculty pay discrepancies by gender or ethnicity. No targets have been set for accountability, and the performance contract negotiation process itself has been done largely behind closed doors.

The only thing that the new performance-based funding scheme ensures is that the public education system will serve the interests of the capitalist class as a whole, while disregarding the general interests of the public at large. The state, as far as higher education is concerned, is being retrofitted for its 19th century function described by Karl Marx and Frederick Engels as "a committee for managing the common affairs of the whole bourgeoisie."

This is a step beyond the exclusivity agreements and corporate partnerships that allow specific corporations to seek special favours on a particular campus or in a particular department. With performance-based funding, *all corporations without discrimination* will get cheap research and will have their human resource requirements fulfilled in the most efficient possible form *by the entire education system*. Over the long haul, if performance-based funding continues in the province of Quebec, we can expect universities to stop producing independent critical thinkers and independent research in the public interest. Simply put, it no longer pays to produce independent critical thought and research.

The success plans forced on Quebec's Cégeps differ from the performance contracts forced on the university system in that they are not negotiated between each individual institution and the MEQ. Nevertheless, they enforce similar standards of market-defined efficiency at the college level. Students who fail to "perform" early on (the same "high risk" groups discriminated against at the university level) will be immediately streamed into terminal programs, while those who meet MEQ standards will be enrolled in university preparatory programs. The wishes of individual students and the special needs of students from different backgrounds will not be allowed to interfere with the efficient production of human resources for the labour market.❖

What are the Ontario government's policy directions concerning higher education?
By Mark Rosenfeld

The government is pursuing funding policy patterns which were evident during its first mandate but which now are more pronounced. There have been limited increases in operating grants, an expansion of tied envelope funding, greater use of matched funding involving the private sector, greater encouragement of college-university-private sector partnerships, and funding linked to performance indicators based on "market principles." There is now also the possibility of a new student-driven funding formula for universities.

Operating grants

Ontario government cutbacks in university funding have significantly exceeded cutbacks in any other province. Operating grants per capita for universities in Ontario are now the lowest of any province in the country. Ontario, Canada's richest province, now spends 38% less per person than the province of Newfoundland on university operating grants, and 18% below the national average. In terms of the four-year relative change in provincial or state funding operating expenses in Canada and the United States between 1995/96 and 1999/2000, Ontario ranks 59th out of the 60 provinces and states.

In March 2000, the government announced transfer payments for 2000/01. Total operating grants were $1.66 billion, an extra $52 million from 2000. More than one-third of that increase was tied funding which was already announced in 1999. The $33 million in "new" funding (a 2% increase) allocated for 2000/01 was tied funding that was based on enrolment growth and university performance. In total, the 3.25% increase in transfer payment funding did not keep pace with inflation and enrolment growth.

The May 2001 Ontario Budget announced that the government would increase operating grants to universities and colleges by $293 million by 2003-04 to accommodate projected increases in enrolment due to demographic changes and the graduation of OAC and Grade 12 students together in 2003 (i.e., the double cohort). By 2003-04, university enrolment is projected to be 16% higher than in 1995, yet funding will have only increased by 7%. Funding per student will be down 8%. If inflation is factored in, then funding per student will have fallen 23% by 2003-04.

In real dollars, government operating grants for the year 2000-01 are still $255 million less than in 1995-96, representing a **shortfall** of 13%. Operating support measured per student has actually declined by $1,300 since 1995-96, representing a drop of 17%.

University-College Administrative Review: "Investing in Students Task Force"

In September 2000, the government announced the establishment of an advisory task force called the Investing in Students Task Force. The task force's stated mandate was "to study college and university administrative operations across the province, examine options for shared services, and identify best practices for administrative functions such as information technology, procurement and data collection."

In March 2001, the task force released its report to the public. The report concluded that universities and colleges **are** efficient in their operations, but $74 to $88 million annually could be saved if recommended changes were adopted across the system. The task force called for an investment of $400 million investment over five years (or $80 million a year) to allow universities and colleges to adopt best practices to achieve those savings.

The underfunding of universities and colleges was clearly observed in the task force report. The report noted that universities have approximately $900 million in deferred maintenance costs. It noted that, between 1990/91 and 2000/01, government operating grants to universities declined by 11% in real dollars, and operating grant revenue per student declined by 29%.

The task force acknowledged that the student demand on the system is going to be dramatic in this decade. It observed that new money will be needed to accommodate the projected enrolment surge, large-scale faculty retirements, deferred maintenance, and new technology. The task force estimated that, by 2005/06, **$351 million will have to be added to university base operating funds to meet needs.** This estimate does not include revenue required to deal with inflation, needed investment to match that of competing jurisdictions, to maintain physical plant nor deal with new and emerging needs such as improved student services or information technology to support innovation.

Recent cutbacks

In November 1999, the government announced $309 million cuts in its projected spending for the next year as a first stage in plans to reduce spending by $900 million within two years. In its announcement, however, the government only outlined $145 million of the reductions to take place in the year 2000. Cuts to post-secondary education totalled almost $30 million.

A breakdown of the spending reductions for post-secondary education is as follows:

Student assistance

The largest portion of the cuts to post-secondary education, **$16.3 million**, came from tightening regulations on student loans. Changes to the student assistance program have resulted in fewer student financial assistance recipients. These changes include tougher credit screening and eligibility requirements for student loans, reassessment of loan eligibility for students who earn more than they state on their loan applications, and lowering the default rate threshold at which institutions must share the costs of student loan defaults. The default rate threshold for 2000-01 is 28.5%, and 25% in 2001-02. Institutions have the option of sharing the default costs for programs above the threshold or removing the high default programs from OSAP eligibility.

The Ontario government's expenditures on student support has dropped from $400 million in 1995-96 to $310 million in 2000-01. Over that same period, the number of student aid recipients in Ontario has decreased by 25%, from 212,000 to 159,000.

Targeted envelopes and matched private sector funding

During its first mandate, the government made extensive use of targeted funding, with provisions for matched private sector contributions, while at the same time it reduced general operating grants. In constant dollar terms, operating grants from the government in 2000-01 are 24.6% lower than in 1992-93. The intention was to align universities more closely with the government's economic development agenda.

The government has used the levers of targeted funding to steer the direction of university education towards a greater emphasis on vocational training and away from the concept of higher education, providing students with the ability to think critically and acquire broad-based knowledge which has both social and economic value. This direction erodes university autonomy and the ability to plan academic programs on a rational basis. University funding tied too closely to industry and business can distort the goals of university research and teaching, and undermine academic freedom.

In the case of matched envelope funding, not all institutions have had the same ability to raise funds, which consequently places some institutions, particularly smaller universities, at a disadvantage.

Funding formula

In its first mandate, the government did not change the university funding formula distribution mechanism, though it did provide funding to address some of the inequities in the funding formula. The government, however, is in favour of promoting greater "market behaviour" in the higher education sector, and it is not inconceivable that it would intervene to change the grant distribution system to promote this objective. Already, the majority of new operating grant funding for 2001-02 is tied to increases in student enrolment (i.e., through the Accessibility Fund).

The Ontario Jobs and Investment Board Report advised the government to consider longer-term alternatives to the current funding formula, such as a student-driven (i.e., consumer-driven) funding system, to replace some or all of the province's grants to colleges and universities. Essentially, this would appear to mean a funding system based on student vouchers.

Capital

In the 1999 and 2000 Ontario Budgets, the government's SuperBuild Growth Fund has provided universities and colleges with a total of $1.2 billion, primarily for new capital projects to accommodate projected student demand. The government claims that this funding, combined with private sector contributions, will create 73,000 new university and college spaces.

Almost three-quarters of the funding under the SuperBuild program is directed to projects in the applied technology, health sciences and general sciences, even though students in liberal arts programs constitute the largest area of university program demand. In each of the last 10 years, more than 40% of applicants have sought access to programs in the arts. The SuperBuild fund does little to support the needs of these students.

Funding for maintaining the existing university infrastructure has been very limited. The government's own Investing in Students Task Force 2001 report identified $900 million in deferred maintenance at universities and $300 million at colleges. The funding provided by government is not keeping pace with the deterioration of buildings.

Tuition

Between 1995 and 2001-02, the government allowed average university tuition fees to increase by more than 60%. The government also allowed deregulation of fees for graduate and certain professional programs, including Business/Commerce (secondary-entry programs), Dentistry, Law, Optometry, Pharmacy and Veterinary Medicine. Fees for undergraduate engineering and computer science programs are to be deregulated following ministerial approval of a university's plans to double the number of entry-level spaces in these programs by September 2000. The government is now considering expanding its policy of tuition deregulation to all undergraduate arts and science programs.

Tuition fees as a proportion of university revenue are at an historically high level. This has important implications for the accessibility and affordability of higher education. In 1997/98 (most recent figures), university income from tuition represented 37.6% of university revenue (57.3% came from operating grants and 5.1% came from other sources). The proportion of university revenue represented by tuition is even higher at some individual universities, and has increased since 1996/97.

Since 1985-86, tuition fees for Bachelor of Arts and Science programs in Ontario universities have increased from $1,215 per year to $4,030 per year in 2001-02.

The impact of these policies has been that the average student debt load has more than doubled since 1995. The government's own Investing in Students Task Force 2001 report noted that the debt load for a four-year BA graduate receiving OSAP was $20,500 (in 1998/99). A May 2001 poll by Ipsos-Reid found that 70% of parents are concerned that their kids won't be able to attend university of college even if they are qualified; 79% (including 78% of decided PC voters) say they can't afford it.

Private universities

In October 2001, the government proclaimed the *Post-secondary Education Choice and Excellence Act, 2000* (Bill 132), which permits private for-profit and non-profit universities to offer degree programs in Ontario. The government has stated that these universities would not receive public operating or capital funding, but that students would be eligible for publicly-funded student assistance to a maximum of $4,500 per year, the same as with publicly-supported institutions. The government claims that private universities will offer greater choice to students, enhance competition with public universities, and improve accessibility to higher education.

Most Ontarians do not see private universities as a solution to the issue of accessibility to higher education. A May 2001 Ipsos-Reid poll found that only 16% of those surveyed supported the expansion of private universities as the solution to accommodate the projected large increase in student demand. In contrast, 64% supported an increase in government funding for public universities.

Private universities are not a solution to the real pressures now facing higher education: an expected 40% increase in university enrolment, a looming faculty shortage crisis, and the impact of years of government underfunding of universities are important issues. Private universities will not ensure improved access to higher education, nor is the quality of the education offered assured. Moreover, the experience of other countries shows that private for-profit universities do receive public funds used to subsidize their profits. In the United States, private post-secondary institutions get 30% of their income from direct and indirect government subsidies.

Accountability, performance indicators, and performance-based funding

The 2001 Ontario Budget announced that the government will create a Public Sector Accountability Act,

proposed in its previous mandate, which will require public sector organizations, including universities, colleges, hospitals, municipalities, school boards, and social service agencies to:
- balance their budgets each year;
- publicly report their annual business plans and how well they performed against these plans; and
- meet minimum (yet to be determined) requirement to ensure they are accountable to the public.

An Accountability Office will be established in the Ministry of Finance "to ensure that transfer payment partners are providing value for taxpayer's money.

The government introduced new performance-based funding for universities in March 2000, and modified the distribution for the fund in 2001. These funds consist of two envelopes:

1) An <u>Accessibility Fund</u> distributed on the basis of enrolment growth each year. According to the government's announcement, universities are only able to access the fund if their admissions to first-year entry-level programs in the fall of the current year are equal to or greater than those for the Fall of the previous year.

   Universities will not receive any money from the enrolment-based Accessibility Fund if they do not increase their first-year enrolment. It would appear that the government wants to make it financially punitive for universities which threaten to limit enrolment in the absence of increased basic operating funds. As well, the government wants universities to expand high-tech and applied science programs based on its narrow reading of the labour market. The Accessibility Fund is therefore seen as another mechanism to steer universities in this direction, in conjunction with other new funding directed to these disciplines. Universities specializing in the liberal arts and, as a result of demographic patterns, universities in certain geographic regions, particularly northern Ontario, could have the greatest difficultly accessing this fund.

2) A <u>Performance Indicator Fund</u> distributed on the basis of institutional performance in the following three indicators: the graduation rate of new first year students; the six-month employment rate of graduates of undergraduate programs; and the two-year employment rate of graduates of undergraduate programs in a selected year. The method of calculating performance funding has been changed from 2000-01. A benchmark has been set at 10% below the system average for the three indicators. Institutions at or above their benchmark will receive funding in proportion to their performance from the benchmark and their size. Institutions below the benchmark will not receive funding.

   (There are many factors which contribute to the employment success of graduates over which universities have no control, such as the state of the local or general economy.)

The recent survey of graduation rates showed greater variation among universities, ranging from 46.3% to 90% among universities. However, graduation rates are influenced by admission policies and types of programs, as well as the type and amount of resources a university can devote to a student's education. Those resources depend on government funding policies. Students who transfer from one university to another also show up on the survey as drop-outs. Graduation rates are a poor and misleading indicator of university performance. The performance indicator tied to the degree completion rate could have the perverse effect of universities lowering standards to boost their completion rate standings.

Student assistance and accessibility

Average student debt load doubled between 1995 and 1999. In 1998-99, the average student debt load for those borrowing on the Ontario Student Assistance Program was $20,496 for a university graduate with a four-year BA degree. The government has paid more attention to the issue of student loan defaults and the issue of isolated "student loan fraud." Post-secondary institutions whose 1997 loan default rate was 15% or more above the provincial average of 23.5% are now required to share the cost of these defaults. The default rate threshold for 33.5% for 1999/2000, 28.5% for 2000-01, and 25% in 2001-02.

The May 2001 Budget stated that, under the Access to Opportunities Program (ATOP), with a $228 million investment in the first three years of the program, the government plans to create 23,000 new spaces for students in computer science and high-demand engineering programs. The private sector has contributed another $136 million to this program, which prepares students for careers in high-demand areas in the economy.

It would appear that, in its second mandate, the student assistance policy direction of the government will continue to be on matched private sector funding, increased university spending on student assistance, and discipline-specific scholarships. The government has stated that every willing and qualified Ontario student will be able to attend a college or university, but has not concretely spelled out how it will alleviate the problem of student debt load or the financial needs of the large influx of students expected over the next decade.

Faculty and staff shortages

The PriceWaterhouseCoopers study commissioned by the Council of Ontario Universities found that between 11,000 and 13,000 new and additional faculty will need to be hired to keep pace with enrolment growth, replace the large number of faculty who will be retiring, and reduce the student faculty ratio to the national average.

To date, the government has not adequately addressed the issue of faculty "renewal"—i.e., faculty shortages in the future or the existing loss of some 2,000 full-time equivalent faculty since 1990-91. The number of faculty has declined by almost 2,000 or 15% since 1990, while enrolment has increased by 6.5%. The current and projected future loss of faculty and staff has major implications, for example, concerning the quality of university teaching and research, faculty workload, and the loss of faculty to other jurisdictions. Ontario universities currently have the highest ratio of full-time equivalent students to full-time faculty in the country. ❖

Manitoba
By Chris Dooley and Todd Scarth

For a decade, Manitobans endured a provincial government that was overtly hostile to public post-secondary education. Under this régime, the system suffered immensely. University enrolments dropped, libraries acquisitions plummeted, and buildings crumbled. Community colleges were left unable to meet the labour market demand, creating wide openings for the private scoter deliver of vocational education. Universities suffered not just program cuts but the consequences of a demoralized teaching community, a problem exacerbated by a bitter labour dispute with the University of Manitoba Faulty Association on 1995. In the late 1990s, they haemorrhaged tenured faculty as many faculty members had taken advantage of early retirement incentive plans designed to reduce payrolls.

A change in government in 1999 has ushered in a somewhat renewed sense of hope in the PSE community. Enrolments are up, tuition fees are down, and the siege mentality that so long prevailed in the system has lifted slightly.

This renewed sense of optimism masks the fact that the problems that plagued the post-secondary education system in the 1990s have not gone away. Despite increases in operating and capital grants, the system is still badly underfunded and probably still losing ground. Although there have been some progressive changes in student aid, including the re-introduction of bursary programs, levels of indebtedness continue to climb and living allowances are barely adequate. A high profile tuition rebate program has certainly helped to increase enrolments, but participation by non-traditional student groups has probably not risen at the same rate as general enrolment.

Accessibility and tuition fees

In September of 1999, Manitoba's current New Democratic government was elected on a platform of five promises. One of these was the promise to increase accessibility to post-secondary education by reducing tuition fees at the province's post secondary institutions by 10%. In practice, this program has had two components, best understood as a tuition freeze and a tuition rebate. For 2000-1, the government has mandated that the universities and post-secondary institutions maintain base tuition fees at 1999 levels, a directive that was renewed for 2001-2. In addition to this tuition freeze, the government has provided what amounts to a 10% tuition voucher to every student. When a student enrols at a Manitoba university of college, fees are assessed at the 1999 level, and the 10% credit is applied "at the wicket." The loss of revenue to the institutions is later offset by a transfer from the provincial government to the post-secondary institution.

By most accounts, the government's tuition fee program has been a resounding success. Overall enrolment rates at Manitoba's post-secondary institutions have gone up by more than 5% in each of the two years that the program has been in place. Manitobans have clearly bought in to the government's "hope for young people" message. The problem is that while tuition cuts may make good politics, they are no more than that unless they are grounded in some type of informed policy.

The principal problem with the government's tuition fee rebate program is that it remains an *ad hoc* initiative. This means that students and potential students must wait until the presentation of the provincial budget every spring to find out whether the tuition policy has been renewed, or whether they might be facing a sudden increase in costs. The government has been very careful to separate the two components of the program, which offers it the maximum room to manouevre and opens the door to cancel one or another component down the line.

Moreover, the 10% reduction from 1999 is purely arbitrary, unsupported by a clearly articulated policy on accessibility which takes into account the real costs of post-secondary education and other determinants of accessibility. At the time the promise was made, the province was clearly suffering a crisis in post-secondary participation. Manitoba had the lowest overall PSE participation rate in the country. Available research suggested strongly that by the mid-1990s, tuition rates had crossed the threshold of deterrence for many prospective students and enrolments were declining at precisely the point in the labour market cycle when one would have anticipated that they would have been on the rise.

The tuition fee promise of 1999 sent a clear message to potential university students that the government wanted them to be able to pursue advanced education, and to do so affordably. Enrolments increased. During the mini-boom of 1999-2001, at a time when Manitoba's labour market was the most competitive that it had been in decades, post secondary participation was on the rise.

Three years later, the problems associated with the 1999 promise are starting to show. The emphasis on annually renewed tuition cuts has substituted for a comprehensive policy that takes into account other determinants of accessibility. Moreover, the government-mandated tuition freeze is beginning to take its toll on the institutions.

While the provincial estimates seem to show significant year over year increases in operating grants, most of the increase has flowed directly to students, not the institutions that they attend. In 2000, for example, about two thirds of the increase in operating grants to the university system was taken up in compensating universities for the tuition rebates. After inflation is accounted, university operating funding was effectively frozen. Given that the system suffered an effective 13% cut in the purchasing power of total allocations from the province through the 1990s, an effective freeze in operating grants is insufficient to prevent the institutions from continuing to lose ground. As a consequence of continued under-funding, library acquisitions continue to drop, and faculty positions continue to sit vacant.

Student aid

Financial Aid to students is another area where Manitobans have seen some progressive change in recent years. The province has continued the $6 million Manitoba Bursary Program that it launched in 2000, the first such program to operate since the previous provincial bursary program was shut down in 1992. This program assists 2,600 students with awards averaging $2,300. This is in addition to $11 million provided through the federal government Millennium Scholarship program, administered in Manitoba as the Manitoba Millennium Bursary Fund. Taken together, these programs provide assistance to approximately 5,500 students.

The province has also started to put money back into provincial ACCESS programs. These programs were established in the late 1980s to provide support for non-traditional students. The original ACCESS programs provided special opportunity grants to Aboriginal people, inner city residents and others. These grants were combined with access to provincial student aid and special counselling and support services which were intended to assist students in the adjustment and acculturation to the university environment. These programs became a model for the rest of Canada, but they too were badly cut back in the 1990s.

Manitoba also garnered guarded praise when it re-directed expenditures previously allocated to the Manitoba Learning Tax Credit program. This was a refundable provincial income tax credit calculated as a percentage of gross tuition costs. Critics charged that the tax credit was regressive and moreover that it was of limited value in increasing accessibility because the credit arrived arrives long after the student has already had to raise the money to pay for tuition. In its 2001 budget, the province cut spending on this credit from approx $15 m to approx $11 m. To the extent that this is a shift of resources to grants, bursaries, or the ACCESS program, it is a progressive move. However, it appears that only about half of the funds cut from the tax credit went to loans, bursaries, or debt forgiveness. Total spending on all grants programs, including the tax credit, fell by $1 million from $47 million last year, as the table below shows.

1.4 million was allocated in the 01-02 budget for the "Post-Secondary Strategic Initiatives Fund," which provides money for the targeted expansion of university and community college programs. This is in addition to $11 million for the Colleges Expansion Initiative that has been and will continue to be used to provide additional spaces and infrastructure for community colleges, in particular the Registered Nurse diploma program.

The Manitoba Student Financial Assistance Branch also administers the federal special opportunity grants program (recently re-named as the Canada Study Grants Program). Grants amounts are as follows:

1. Canada Study Grants for Full-time Students with Dependents: The maximum is $40/week for students with 1 to 2 dependents; $60/week for students with 3 or more dependents. This grant is awarded when need exceeds $275/week, and is automatically assessed when the student applies for Canada/Manitoba Student Loan.

2. Canada Study Grants for Part-time Students with Dependents: Assistance is intended for part-time students who have an assessed need after receiving the maximum High-need Grant for Part-time students ($1,200) and maximum part-time Canada Student Loan of $4,000. Students who apply for Part-time Canada Student Loan are automatically assessed for the high-need grant and the Canada Study Grant.

3. Canada Study Grants for Students with Permanent Disabilities: Assistance of up to $5,000 is available to cover the exceptional education-related costs associated with permanent disabilities. Applicants must provide verification of their disability and a detailed cost-estimate.

Canada Study Grants for Female Doctoral Students: The current maximum is up to $3,000 per year for up to three years. This assistance is provided only for certain fields of study, and students must be taking studies at the doctoral (PhD) level.

Grants programs etc. in the provincial budget estimates for 2001/2

Total Loans and Bursaries	$9.3 million
Interest Relief and Debt Reduction	$1.8 million
Manitoba Scholarships and Bursaries Initiative:	$5 million
Manitoba Learning Tax Credit	$10.8 million
Canada Study Grants:	$2.1 million
Canada Millennium Scholarship Fund	$11.0 million
Manitoba Millennium Bursary Fund	$6.0 million
Total:	$46 million

Quality of education

The biggest problem facing Manitoba's post-secondary institutions is a revenue problem. After inflation is accounted, university operating funding has been effectively frozen. Given that the system suffered an effective 13% cut in the purchasing power of total allocations from the province through the 1990s, an effective freeze in operating grants is insufficient to prevent the institutions from continuing to lose ground.

This has brought the provincial government and the University of Winnipeg into open conflict. The University of Winnipeg, as a result of the way in which it assesses students, is more reliant on tuition fees than the province's other universities and receives a smaller effective *per capita* grant from the province. The university is facing a fiscal crisis which it blames in part on the tuition freeze, and is threatening to operate at a deficit — which it is prohibited to do by law — rather then compromise quality of education. At the time of writing the outcome of this conflict is undetermined, but it brings into sharp focus the perils of freezing tuition, the system's second most important revenue source, without adequate compensation.

The University of Winnipeg's position has merit, but the crisis that it faces is probably more correctly attributed to a long-term under-funding than to the recent tuition freeze. It would appear that the province's post-secondary institutions have actually benefited financially form the increased enrolments. The government has funded the tuition freeze with increases in operating grants, and in most instances, the additional students have been accommodated without the requirement of additional capital and operating expenditure.

Moreover the government has been seeking creative ways to flow more money to post-secondary institutions. In the summer of 2000, it attempted to flow a non-recurring surplus for the publicly-owned auto insurance corporation to PSE infrastructure initiatives, but the initiative turned into a public-relations nightmare and the government was forced to back-down. More recently, the government indicated that would exempt post-secondary institutions from paying municipal property taxes. This replaces about $20 million that was taken away from the university system in the mid-1990s when the Filmon government chose to stop paying grants in lieu of taxes to the municipalities, a move that had the same effect as cutting about $18 million from the operating grants to the universities.

The biggest problem is that the cuts of the 1990s are simply too big to make up without a very large infusion of new money. When the current government took office, Manitoba had the lowest rate of post-secondary funding per capita of any province in Canada and it showed. The public community college system was in a shambles, and between 1993-4 and 1996-7, the province lost 11% of its full-time university faculty (13% at the university of Manitoba). In roughly the same period, the university libraries cancelled roughly 40% of its periodical subscriptions. The results, already observable in a decline in the graduate student population, has been an overall loss in research and teaching capacity.

Moreover, the province's post secondary institutions are facing an accumulated infrastructure deficit of on the order of $200 million. To be fair, the current government has increased the capital budgets for post-secondary institutions, and it has undertaken to construct a second campus for badly overcrowded the Red River Community College, but much more is required to make up for the cuts of the previous decade.

Conclusion

In the end, the government of Manitoba is doing most things right. It has shown a genuine commitment to making post-secondary education more accessible, through reductions in tuition, replacement of monies previously cut from targeted accessibility programs and through

The biggest problem that the government faces is that it is operating in a very small box, in part one of its own making. This fiscal year the government cut net taxes by $185 million — thus further reducing a revenue base already eroded by losses in federal transfers. This has left it unwilling and unable to consider taking on the most basic issue that faces post-secondary institutions: that the base level of funding was dropped below the threshold of sustainability.❖

Post-secondary education in Saskatchewan

By James M. Pitsula

The year can be characterized as one of moderate funding increases to post-secondary education, increases that were not sufficient to avert major tuition hikes at the universities and the Saskatchewan Institute for Applied Science and Technology (SIAST). The Department of Post-Secondary Education and Skills Training continued the development of a sector strategic plan, which emphasized, among other items, technology-enhanced learning and Aboriginal access to higher education.

The overall impression was one of government, universities, institutes, and colleges trying to work collaboratively on a plan for the advancement of higher education in the province, but doing so in a context of limited financial resources. As a result, students had to bear a larger share of the cost of their education.

Provincial budget

The Saskatchewan budget for 2001-2002 provided a 3.5% increase in the operating grants of the province's two universities. In addition, $3 million was set aside for allocation according to the Saskatchewan Universities Funding Mechanism, a new formula for the division of grants to the universities arising from the 1998 DesRosiers Report. In 2000 DesRosiers submitted a supplementary report that included more detailed calculations.

The contents of the reports continue to be the subject of discussion between the government and the two universities. When the reports are finally implemented, they will determine the basis of university funding, but in the meantime, only a portion of the budget increment (the aforesaid $3 million) was apportioned under the new mechanism. In the end, $2.4 million of the $3 million was given to the University of Saskatchewan, the balance going to St. Thomas More College at the University of Saskatchewan campus and Luther College at the University of Regina campus. Details of the new funding mechanism continue to be discussed through 2001-2002, with a view to full implementation in 2002-2003. Whether the transition occurs on schedule remains to be seen.

In addition to the 3.5% increase to operating grants and the $3 million allocated under the new funding formula, the government announced two specific funding initiatives. A total of

$500,000 was provided for undergraduate entrance scholarships, $150,000 going to the University of Regina and $350,000 to the University of Saskatchewan. The grant was contingent upon the universities matching the amount from internal sources, thereby securing an overall increase of $1,000,000 for undergraduate scholarships. Both universities decided to allocate even more than the amount required to match the grant. The University of Regina allocated $200,000 for student support and another $200,000 enhancement of graduate student funding. The University of Saskatchewan provided $500,000 for undergraduate scholarships and bursaries.

The other targeted grant contained in the provincial budget was $1.5 million for information technology programs, with the specific goal of "helping to meet the urgent need for additional Information Technology professionals in Saskatchewan." Of this amount, $625,000 went to the University of Regina and $875,000 to the University of Saskatchewan. This expenditure was in keeping with a long-term objective of the government to assist the application of technology to learning.

The grant for SIAST increased 3.9%, bringing its total operating budget to $61,072,000. On the capital side, spending for the entire post-secondary education sector was down slightly, falling from $31,830,000 to $29,830,000. Overall, the post-secondary budget, including universities, SIAST, regional colleges, training programs, employment centres, student aid, the Department's own operations, etc., rose from $494,066,000 in 2000-2001 to $511,486,000 in 2001-2002, a gain of 3.5%.

Tuition fees and student support

Despite provincial funding increases, both universities found it necessary to raise tuition fees. The University of Regina's increase was 8.95% and that of the University of Saskatchewan 15%. Tuition fees at SIAST increased 9% in accordance with a plan to make tuition constitute 20% of the total cost of technical education, instead of the current 13%. The plan is to increase tuition at SIAST by 9% in each of the next three years.

As a result of university tuition fee increases, Saskatchewan is positioned somewhat below Alberta, but higher than Manitoba. For an Arts student, the annual tuition rate at the University of Manitoba was $3,093, compared with University of Alberta, $3,975; University of Calgary, $3,890; University of Saskatchewan, $3,790; and University of Regina, $3,573. For a Science student, the figures were: University of Manitoba, $3,650; University of Alberta, $3,975; University of Calgary, $3,890; University of Saskatchewan, $3,860; and University of Regina, $3,684. Despite rising tuition costs, the university participation rate in Saskatchewan remained fairly high, with 24% of the province's 18-24-year-olds enrolled full-time in university.

It should also be mentioned in connection with student financial support that in February 2001 the government announced the establishment of a new five-year Centennial Summer Student Employment program (the Centennial in question being that of the Province of Saskatchewan in 2005). In 2001-2002, the universities and federated colleges received up to $4,000 per student to provide career-related summer jobs.

The major change to student loans was the announcement in June 2001 of the integration of the Canada Student Loans Program with the Government of Saskatchewan Student Financial Assistance Program. This administrative simplification means that students now have one loan and one repayment. The existing financing agreement for student loans with the Royal Bank of Canada ended on July 31, 2001. After that date the government again became the lender, as it had been before the signing of the five-year agreement with the bank.

In the period from August 1, 2001 to December 31, 2001, 14,200 Saskatchewan students were authorized to receive $51.3 million in financial assistance (loans and bursaries). This compares with 14,713 students authorized to receive $52.2 million in the same period in the previous year. The drop conforms to a trend over the past few years of declining totals for student financial assistance. The cause of the decline is not clear, except that it has occurred at a time when the number of applicants for financial assistance has increased. It seems that more applicants come from families whose incomes are too high for them to be eligible for loans.

Other significant developments

The main developments in the field of post-secondary education were continued work on the phase-in of the Saskatchewan Universities Funding Mechanism, the publication of *A Progress Report on University Revitalization*, and the drafting of the Department of Post-Secondary Education and Skills Training *Sector Strategic Plan*. The *Progress Report* was an update on the implementation of the government's fall 1996 report titled *Public Interest and Revitalization of Saskatchewan's Universities*, which was the government's response to the MacKay Report.

The *Progress Report* noted that both universities have established strategic planning processes. The University of Saskatchewan's emphasis was on being nationally competitive with other universities in the medical-doctoral category, with a focus on Biotechnoloy, Environmental Sciences, Health Sciences, Identity and Diversity, Material Science, and Technology and Change. The University of Regina identified five focus areas: Culture and Heritage, Energy and the Environment, Informatics, Population Health, and Social Justice. This was to fulfill the Provincial Government's desire that each university carve out its own niche of research and service to the community and avoid unnecessary duplication.

The Department of Post-Secondary Education's *Strategic Plan* gave high priority to the adoption of technology to enable students in rural and northern areas to take distance-education and on-line courses, and made targeted funds available for this purpose. The universities are working with the Department to develop a website, *Campus Saskatchewan*, which is intended to be a searchable database of all resources available to Saskatchewan learners.

Increasing Aboriginal access to post-secondary education was another top priority in strategic planning. A major development was the commencement of construction of a new building for Saskatchewan Indian Federated College in the northeast corner of the University of Regina campus. The four-storey, 139,160-square-foot building has a semi-circular structure symbolic of the Sundance Lodge tradition. Given that for 24 years the classrooms and offices of the college have been scattered in rented facilities across Regina, the new building of striking design and profile represents a leap forward for Aboriginal education in Saskatchewan. In addition, the federal government in 2001-2002 provided $3 million in funding for a new Institute of Aboriginal People's Health, a research initiative led by SIFC in collaboration with the University of Regina and the University of Saskatchewan.

Conclusions

The universities are working cooperatively with each other and the government to use resources efficiently on a province-wide basis. Unfortunately, lack of government funds means that students must pay ever-higher tuition fees, and many of them end up with onerous debt loads.

The provincial government wants to have objective measures of the success of universities in achieving their objectives. An assumption seems to be that education is a process with quantifiable results. The *Progress Report on University Revitalization* states that the goal of post-secondary education is "to provide the Saskatchewan public with relevant, high-quality programs and services, on a cost-effective and sustainable basis."

The problem with "relevance" is that what is relevant today quickly becomes irrelevant tomorrow. Defenders of the traditional university say that nothing is more relevant than studying Plato or Shakespeare, and that the students with a good liberal arts education are best equipped to meet the challenges of the future. In the current political and cultural climate, the emphasis on immediate pay-off for investment in higher education and an exaggerated attention to economic utility leads to the downplaying of traditional university ideals.

The tendency is to see universities as engines driving the economy, rather than as "vital islands of culture and critical thought in a materialistic society." The consequence, unfortunately, is that higher education is not the social priority that it deserves to be.❖

Higher education in Alberta, 2001-2002
By Cameron Graham and Dean Neu

Funding again dominates the discourse on higher education in Alberta. Provincial revenues from non-renewable resources soared in fiscal 2001, bringing the first increase in real-dollar per-student funding for some institutions in more than 20 years. However, this one-time increase in education funding ($0.3 billion) was much lower than the province's increase in revenue ($5.9 billion). In relative terms, education funding went up a healthy 6%, but revenue went up 128%.

The first half of fiscal 2002, however, has seen a global economic downturn and lower natural gas prices. The result has been that provincial revenues, though unchanged from the same period in the previous year, are down more than 20% from anticipated levels. The provincial government has asked for immediate budget cuts in all departments, renewing the pressure on government funding of higher education.

These fluctuations in provincial revenues reveal an asymmetry in the flow of funding. Windfalls in revenue do not lead to commensurate or timely increases in funding for higher education, but lower revenues quickly lead to reduced funding.

The one-year increase in funding in 2001 did little to make up for the decline in real-dollar funding over the previous two decades. This long-term drop in funding has forced the province's universities and colleges to pursue other revenue. The two primary sources they have tapped have been tuition and corporate funding.

Tuition has increased steadily in Alberta since 1990, even during the 2001 revenue boom. The increases announced for 2001 and 2002 were among the lowest in years, but they were still between 3% and 4%. Except for the University of Lethbridge, which froze tuitions at 2001 levels, these increases were well above inflation levels. In addition, the increases for the 2001-2002 academic year were only as small as they were because of a one-time grant from the province. Given the recent drop in provincial resource revenues, this grant is not expected to be repeated.

To offset the impact of provincial funding cuts and to reduce reliance on tuition increases, post-secondary institutions in Alberta have turned to corporate funding sources. Technical institutes, for example, are placing increased emphasis on revenue-generating training programs, tailored to individual corporate clients and funded entirely by them. Many post-secondary institutions are also offering vendor-specific technical certification courses. In addition, corporate sponsorship for classrooms and other facilities has created increased advertising on campuses. Taken together, these changes show how Alberta's post-secondary institutions are being shaped and influenced more and more by the business community.

These changes have also helped align the educational institutions with the provincial government's goals for higher education. These goals include a strong emphasis on economic outcomes. Education is viewed as vocational training, research is viewed as a basis of commercial innovation, and business is seen as the consumer of graduates.

An example of this thinking comes from the website of Alberta Learning, the department of the provincial government responsible for higher education. The website asks the question, "What subjects can I study?" Its immediate answer begins: "If you are planning to work in a specific occupation, or would like more information about career choices before you decide on a field of study..." Alberta Learning, by this evidence, assumes that education is occupation-related.

Much of what Alberta Learning has published in the past year puts a similarly high emphasis on employability and career training. Any intrinsic value of education is played down, and sometimes ignored entirely.

Subtle changes in funding have reinforced this vocational and economic view of education. The proportion of higher education funding devoted to universities has dropped since 1995, relative to technical and vocational institutes. Education in Alberta is in some respects becoming equated with the production of workers.

Less subtle changes have come in the area of accreditation. The provincial government has given an increasing number of technical and community colleges the right to grant degrees in the past few years. Private colleges can obtain degree-granting status by Order in Council, avoiding any debate in the provincial legislature. Furthermore, the accreditation process itself has been weakened, no longer requiring a private college to spend a period of time in affiliation with an Alberta university.

Finally, a new funding regime requires the province's accreditation board to recoup its costs from the applicants, putting private colleges in the position of "customer." The conflict between the need to maintain standards and the need to satisfy customers is obvious, but any measures that may have been taken to address this are less clear.

The provincial government's goals for education are given in the Alberta Learning "Business Plan," which outlines the department's "core business goals." (This adoption of corporate methods and jargon is interesting in its own right.) The overall goal appears to be one of lifelong learning. Alberta Learning encourages diversity and flexibility in education and training programs, including continuing education and part-time programs of study. The outcome measurements for higher education used by Alberta Learning align with the government's economic view of education. The measurements include:

- graduates' satisfaction with post-secondary education (now 79%, target 80%);
- completion rate for programs started by students (now 55%, target 58%);
- employment rates of post-secondary graduates (now 93%);
- public satisfaction with preparedness of graduates for citizenship (now on target at 65%);
- satisfaction of institutional stakeholders with their collaborations with Alberta Learning (various measures in the 70-80% range); and
- percentage of adult Albertans participating in post-secondary education (now 33%, target 36%).

Given this emphasis on economic outcomes for education, it is difficult to say if higher education in Alberta is actually improving or worsening. It is probably more accurate to say that it is being skewed in the direction of corporate-sponsored technical training.

This is consistent with the Alberta government's generally pro-business philosophy. It means that technical training is going to be easier and easier for students to obtain, although at higher tuition costs. Students wishing to pursue an education in arts or sciences are less likely to enjoy such benefits.❖

British Columbia
By Roseanne Moran and Anita Zaenker

British Columbia saw a change of government in 2001. The full impact of the change has yet to be felt as the new government inherited a recently tabled budget when it was elected and has subsequently made few changes to the overall budget, although specific areas are already feeling the effect of a new policy direction.

The new government inherits the same set of factors, however, that will drive continued demand for more access. B.C.'s post-secondary education age cohort will grow substantially over the next several years, while it is declining in many other provinces. Forest and coastal communities will need more support to deal with economic transition as the economy takes a nosedive. The capacity of the new government to deal with this demand, however, is substantially reduced by personal and corporate tax cuts that will drain the provincial treasury of billions.

The new government has launched a cross-government "Core Services Review" aiming at identifying ways to reduce government spending. Amid the review, the government announced its intention to freeze funding at 2001-02 levels for education, post-secondary education and health, while delivering cuts of 30% or more to other parts of government. While the future may be bleak, the B.C. post-secondary system began the year robustly.

The 2001-02 budget brought good news for post-secondary education, including an 8% increase in funding for post-secondary education programs. Prior to the budget, then Premier Ujjal Dosanjh announced a 5% cut in tuition fees and 5,025 new student spaces for 2001-02. Dosanjh also announced a one-time funding increase of $46 million, in addition to that previously allocated in the 2000-01 budget, with $23 million going to the four research universities and $23 million going to the college and institute system to support the purchase of new equipment and library resources.

Specific areas of enrolment growth were targeted within the 2001-02 growth allocation of 5,025 spaces, including additional funding of $11.5 million to create 3,150 more trades and technical training spaces. The B.C. government has set a target of creating 50,000 new apprenticeships over the next four years. Institutions are also required to add 450 new nursing spaces and 500 new spaces in high-tech programs.

The new government has also announced a sweeping nurse recruitment and retention package. The budget included an important addition of $1 million in base funding for library support in university college degree programs.

Tuition fees

Tuition fees at B.C.'s public institutions were reduced by 5% for the 2001-02 academic year. The reduction was legislated in March by the New Democratic government through the "Access to Education Act" and has been implemented by the new B.C. Liberal government. The reduction follows five years of a fee freeze. As a means of getting around the provincial regulation, institutions have introduced new programs on a full-cost-recovery basis. Such programs in 2001-02 included Simon Fraser University's Masters of Business Administration degree.

As promised in the B.C. Liberals' election platform, called the New Era Document, or "N.E.D.," the Ministry of Advanced Education launched its review of "hidden costs" of the tuition fee freeze. The ministry's mandate is to consult with "educators, students and administrators on the hidden costs to students and institutes of previous tuition freezes that were not properly funded by government and that have reduced student access and reduced course offerings." Post-secondary stakeholders have been asked to answer five questions relating to the tuition fee freeze in written submissions and public consultations with the minister.

The minister has indicated that her government's position on tuition fees will be announced in early 2002. Given the public comments of Members of the Legislative Assembly on whether or not government should regulate tuition fees to keep post-secondary education affordable, it appears unlikely that the tuition fee freeze will continue.

Presidents of many post-secondary institutions have actively spoken out against the tuition fee freeze and reduction, saying that it has negatively affected the quality of education.

Student assistance

B.C. remains one of two provinces offering non-repayable study grants in all four years of an undergraduate education. In 2000-01, the B.C. government spent $77 million to provide grants to approximately 26,000 students. As a result, student debt among B.C. students is lower than elsewhere in the country.

The administration of the B.C. Student Loans Program was taken over by B.D.P., a for-profit service provider in July 2000. The administration of the Canada Student Loans Program was taken over by Edulinx in August 2001. As a result, students experienced confusion and incorrect information about the mechanics of applying for and receiving B.C. Student Assistance. Many students encountered delays in receiving funds for September 2001 due to Edulinx's inability to turn around funds within 2-3 days, as per the stated contract.

In July 2001, credit checks were introduced for B.C. applicants for student loans. The government had refused to implement federal policy introduced in 1998 requiring applicants to be credit screened before receiving student loans. However, a change in the federal policy resulted in the province no longer having the option of implementing this policy. Individuals will be required to provide the government with access to their credit records, and those who are deemed in need of financial assistance, but who do not pass the credit check, will be denied access to both the Canada Student Assistance Program and the B.C. Student Assistance Program. The credit check will screen out those applicants who have missed three payments on three debts totalling $1,000 each in the last three years. It is expected that this policy will deny student financial assistance to approximately 200 students in British Columbia.

The B.C. Liberals' New Era Document promised a student-loans forgiveness program for students attending accredited nursing and medical schools who agree to practise in rural, under-served communities. Students graduating after 2001 will have outstanding B.C. student loans forgiven at a rate of 20% per year. In addition, the B.C. government will pay the interest on the student loan for each year of practice. Despite high student debt loads in all programs of study, only nursing and medical students are eligible for loan forgiveness.

There is much speculation that the new government will seek to revamp the student assistance program, particularly if tuition fees are deregulated.

Capital

In recognition of the significant erosion of the physical capacity and condition of the post-secondary education system as a result of an ongoing freeze on major capital and limited funding for minor capital, the 2001-02 budget included capital pre-planning grants to allow institutions to refine the scope and cost of critically necessary major capital projects. A B.C. Fiscal Review Panel appointed by the newly-elected Liberal government documented the extent of the capital crisis in the B.C. post-secondary education system. The panel noted that, for the past several years, the post-secondary sector in B.C. has not proceeded with necessary capital expenditures, instead making increased use of existing facilities.

The fiscal review also identified some $400 million in deferred capital maintenance in the post-secondary education sector and cautioned against the false economy of deferring maintenance to the point where assets begin to deteriorate. Despite this, the Minister of Advanced Education was forced to issue a news release in September confirming news reports that capital projects throughout the province had been cancelled, or at least deferred, in order to make room for new priorities that were part of the Liberal election platform.

Future directions

The new government has initiated a flurry of consultative processes, including a Standing Committee of Education which is scheduled to report to the B.C. Legislature in February 2002.

In November 2001, the Advanced Education Minister received cabinet approval for a series of strategic shifts, along with a nine-point plan. Some of the key directions point to a future with more emphasis on private institutions and private funding, greater interest in online education and performance measures that focus on student success, and new costs for students, whether as a result of more private post-secondary education or higher tuition fees.

The provincial budget, scheduled for Feb. 19, 2002, will hold some surprises, but much of the post-secondary agenda of the new government will have been made public by then. ❖

Editors note: The present Liberal BC government has recently announced the deregulation of tuition fees at BC universities.

Confronting the higher education debates

By Denise Doherty-Delorme and Erika Shaker

What Canadians want

Since its conception in 1999, *Missing Pieces* has examined and critiqued the role of the federal and provincial governments in the status, goals and direction of higher education in Canada. This third report looks at the education system on the basis of what Canadians have repeatedly said are the issues that are important to them.

A 2000 Ekos poll found that 90% of Canadians thought that education should be a high priority with the federal government (second only to health care at 92%).

But, although Canadians clearly want the federal government to take an active leadership role in protecting and enriching higher education, the political rhetoric surrounding PSE is often contradictory. Grandiose commitments to accessibility are followed by funding cuts, tuition fee increases, and, in some cases, outright tuition fee deregulation.

Federal and provincial pledges to maintain quality in educational institutions are offset by the curtailment of academic freedom, rising student-faculty ratios, and inadequate operating budgets. Canadians expect higher education to be of a high quality, accessible and affordable—that it will meet the needs of and be accountable to the public, and be equitably funded and administered.

While the public is told it is entitled to these expectations, the political, legislative and financial constraints placed on universities and colleges seem designed to force that same public to scale back its expectations of higher education.

Political leaders increasingly treat post-secondary education as less a communal and social responsibility than an individual investment—a view that is reinforced in the media. The debate over universal access to higher education has been superseded by a focus on the *individual's* responsibility for ensuring that he or she can afford university or college: the responsibility of parents to invest in RESPs (Registered Education Savings Plans); students working part-time or full-time; students or families personally taking on the responsibility of education-related debts.

This new focus on the responsibility of individuals and families to ensure their access to higher education absolves governments of their responsibility to maintain a high-quality post-secondary education system accessible to all.

Individual vs. social responsibility

When education is seen as an individual responsibility, it fundamentally jeopardizes accessibility—a problem that is apparent now more than ever. At the same time as the federal government was cutting transfer payments to the provinces, the provinces were eliminating student grants and raising tuition fees. That tuition fees have now become a substantial barrier for low- and middle-income students has been documented by many studies done by both students and faculty (*see articles in Missing Pieces II for further details*).

Because of the high personal cost associated with attending a college or university, parental income level is a vital determinant in PSE accessibility. A Statistics Canada study (*The Daily*, Tues. Apr. 10, 2001) found that "parents reported education savings for fewer than 20% of children living in households in which the income was under $30,000. In contrast, in households with incomes of $80,000 or more, parents reported savings for 63% of children."

The survey demonstrated that, in general, parents had saved "nowhere near the estimated amount required to put their children through an entire post-secondary education." This is due in part to tuition fees that have risen 126.2% over the past decade, six times faster than the rate of inflation. Another reason is that half of these education savings are invested in RESPs, and, with fluctuations in the financial markets, they have lost much of their market value over the last few years. As the Canadian Deposit Insurance Corporation keeps reminding us, RESPs are not a secure investment vehicle.

Nor are all families able to save the required amount. "Median savings for each child," says StatsCan, "declined as the number of children in the household increased. In households with only one child, median accumulated savings were $3,600 in 1999. That fell to $3,000 per child in households with three children, and to $2,500 per child where there were four children or more."

And finally, the study concludes with an observation that would seem to be self-evident: "*For all age groups, median savings tended to increase with household income*" (emphasis added). Any federal or provincial policies that require the individual student and his or her parents to shoulder more of the educational bill will restrict access to colleges and universities for many Canadians.

Deconstructing the debates: Existing research

Governments have based their policy decisions in part on a body of research done by some of Canada's right-wing think-tanks and PSE service providers. Much of this research tends to offer up so-called solutions that are merely just a reinforcement of the status quo. Many of the market "solutions" that are suggested by this research rationalize the creation of an elitist higher education system by lowering accessibility and generating profits for the financial institutions that provide student loans and educational savings. Below is a review of some of the recent research done on Canadian post-secondary education and a critique of the findings.

The research that has been undertaken to identify the barriers to the pursuit of higher education tends, alarmingly, to downplay the magnitude of financial barriers to PSE. Most recently, the Millennium Scholarship Foundation's paper by E. Dianne Looker (December 2001, *Why Don't They Go On?: Factors affecting the decision of Canadian youth not to pursue post-secondary education*[1]) serves to camouflage the issue of education funding, student financial aid, rising tuition fees, and student debt. For example, when asked the reasons for not pursuing PSE, the most frequently cited individual reason, in the above-mentioned study, at 23%, was: "did not have enough money to continue." However, the report takes great pains to minimize this figure by asserting that a majority of respondents did *not* cite financial reasons: "A key finding was that most students listed a non-financial reason for not attending PSE—that is, 77% gave reasons other than [did not have enough money to continue]." The emphasis of the report is placed not on the barrier most often cited, but on those respondents who did *not* cite that reason.

Yet several of the "non-financial barriers" to PSE cited by Looker's paper actually have an underlying economic and financial basis. For example, "taking time off from studying" (at 19%) is often related to needing to work in order to make money to pay for higher education. A "lack of interest in pursuing higher education" may be influenced by socioeconomic background, especially when the level of the parents' education is considered.

This was found to be true in the *Youth in Transition Survey*, 2002 (HRDC and Statistics Canada). High school dropouts (aged 18 to 20) are twice as likely to come from a single-parent family and three times as likely to have parents who had not finished high school themselves. Both of these groups are likely to be at a lower socioeconomic level. This high dropout rate is even more alarming when it is noted that nearly half of all high school leavers had a B average or better. Furthermore, half of all 18-to-20-year-old university and college students had to maintain a part-time job while attending school, and just over 10% had to maintain full-time employment.

"Other" reasons (at nearly 13%) form a considerable group of respondents in the Looker study, but are lumped in as specifically non-financial.

One of the conclusions drawn in the Foundation's report is that, "although securing access to PSE for all Canadians may involve more than just financial assistance, we cannot ignore the

Barriers to Post-secondary education

	High School Dropouts, no PSE	High school continuers	High school graduates, no PSE	PSE continuers	PSE graduates	PSE leavers	All
% of 18-20-year olds	10.4	13.0	22.7	45.3	3.7	4.9	100
% reporting facing barriers to "going as far in school as would like to"	60.7	42.6	51.3	40.6	42.9	49.7	45.9
% reporting a financial barrier	53.1	56.6	70.7	68.9	70.4	71.4	65.9

Source: HRDC, Statistics Canada. *At a Crossroads: First results for the 18-to 20-year-old cohort of the Youth in Transition Survey*, January 2002.

barriers posed by affordability. Being able to afford PSE will likely remain a hurdle for many young people; the evidence... suggests, however, that in many cases there are other hurdles to be overcome first [p 34], (p6)." This in spite of an earlier conclusion that the individual 'hurdle' most frequently cited by youth *is* a lack of money. Once again, the significance of financial barriers is minimized, justifying the decision not to address the negative impact of tuition fees and student debt.

Looker further summarizes the evidence by again minimizing—or at least decontextualizing—the financial barriers to pursuing an education. The quotation below demonstrates how social issues are separated from economic ones:

> "One of the interesting things revealed... is the important role that *non-financial* factors played in the decision about how much education to take. Attitudes about oneself and one's abilities, confidence levels, attitudes to formal schooling, preferred and expected jobs, and levels of certainty (or uncertainty) about the future all played a role. Friends, family, and school officials also played a part in providing either incentives or disincentives to further education."

The implication that self-esteem, attitudes (family or personal) to formal schooling, and preferred or expected jobs have no relationship to financial status is unrealistic. But it appears to form the underpinning of the conclusions of this report:

> "The oft-cited economic advantages of having a post-secondary education are not likely to persist if most Canadians have some sort of PSE credential. Rather, the effect would be to transform post-compulsory education into education compulsory for employment. In that scenario, employers would have to look for other markers when choosing employees.
>
> "While recognizing the non-economic benefits of PSE, so long as there are jobs that do not require

PSE, it makes little sense to push everyone to prolong their education. It needs to be recognized that individuals can find other ways of obtaining a viable and sustainable living besides getting a post-secondary credential."

The intent of the report is somewhat fuzzy here. Is the author implying that eliminating financial barriers to PSE will in fact diminish the importance of higher education because there will be more university and college graduates? Or is she suggesting that the job-related benefits are diminished by the public's accessibility to higher education?

Looker concludes that it is primarily parental education—not financial and other factors—that affect PSE attendance patterns. Yet it is a misconception to imply that the level of parental education (or emphasis on higher education) is unrelated to income; the report therefore does not adequately examine the degree to which income is both a direct and indirect factor in an individual's decision to pursue higher education.

We believe that it is a fundamental responsibility of a democratic society to provide to all its members the opportunity to pursue higher education if, when, and where they choose. And we continue to believe that it is irresponsible for a society to educate its citizens while at the same time burdening them to such a degree with student debt that they may not be able to pursue the careers for which they were educated and trained. So the question remains as to how much personal debt is acceptable in order to obtain an education.

Acceptable levels of debt?

Students, their families and student groups have maintained that school leavers of the last decade have been saddled with an inordinate amount of debt. A 1996 HRDC report, *Take on the Future: Canadian Youth and the World of Work*, estimated the average student debt load after completion of a four-year program to be $25,000. Since that report, federal or provincial governments have not conducted comprehensive[2] research to accurately assess the level of debt associated with higher education.

This is partly because policy-makers continue to debate ways to accurately portray the "average" debt holder. This can include factoring non-borrowers into the equation when attempting to determine the average debt load of students and graduates. But including non-borrowers simply masks the real overall effect of the student aid. Student aid is designed specifically for those students who are unable to meet the financial requirements of attending a college or university. It is this group that must be exclusively addressed to determine the impact of student aid policy, not those for whom student aid is not required.

Another example of strategic data selection—or the absence of up-to-date data—is seen in the C.D. Howe Institute's November 2001 *Commentary* titled *Measuring the Load, Easing the Burden*, by Ross Finnie. An acceptable level of debt, Finnie contends, is equivalent to "some of the least expensive new cars available for sale," approximately $13,000. What the one has to do with the other is never explained. An acceptable level of debt, as any good banker will explain, can only be based on current assets and income, but the vast majority of students have neither assets nor income, and so for them no level of education-related debt is acceptable.

The C.D. Howe *Commentary* suggests simply expanding the current student loans system, rather than a wholesale increase in grants or lowering tuition fees. This conclusion is based on the limited data found in the *National Graduate Survey of the Class of 1995* (done by Statistics Canada). The class of 1995 largely consists of university undergraduates who would have had loans from the late 1980s and the early 1990s, thus leaving school with, on average, $10,000 in student loan debt. Finnie postulates that "An updating of the record to the present would likely yield only moderate changes to this profile". Yet, just five years later, the average debt had reached almost $14,000. If we extrapolate this debt increase over the next seven years, we can hypothesize that 2002 school leavers could have an average debt load of $23,800.

But this is only the average of *government* student loan debt; it does not take other forms of debt or the interest charged on students loans into account. Many students must borrow from other sources (parents, spouse, private bank loans) in order to pay all of their educational expenses. Interest charged on student loans can be as high as the prime rate plus another 5%. Over the course of repayment, these high interest rates can easily increase the student loan by another 50%. Therefore, a student graduating in 2002 can expect to repay on average $35,700. But many are forced to incur much higher debts. It is not unheard-of to find school leavers owing as much as $100,000.

This C.D. Howe *Commentary* concludes by suggesting that "Each principal stakeholder—the federal government, provincial governments, and students themselves—put an additional $1,000 per capita into the system. Students would pay their share through increased tuition, but those who needed aid would receive assistance through grants and the enhanced loans program proposed in this *Commentary*." This simplistic solution, however, only serves to increase student loans and debt loads, since it fails to offer an increase in student grants. Students in 2002 are already paying much more than an additional $1,000 in fees for their education than students who started at the beginning of the decade. On average, students in the fall of 2001 paid $3,452 in tuition fees, which is over 100% higher than the average of $1,714 paid in 1991.

One of the other areas that policy-makers must consider is the effect of student loan debt on the lives of students and their families. We urge the federal government to look closely at the impact that tuition fees, debt and interest charges have, not just on students, but on all those affected by an inaccessible and unaffordable system of education.

Equality of opportunity in education and research

Policies limiting accessibility to higher education impact equity-seeking groups in different ways.[3] The Assembly of First Nations has been vocal about its concern with rising tuition fees. When fees rose in 2001, Indian and Northern Affairs Canada did not increase post-secondary funding; this limits the number of First Nations students who can attend school (because budgets are capped at the First Nations level).

The ways in which targeted funding is affecting the quality and accountability of university and college education is also inadequately examined. There is a need to evaluate the roles of the Canadian Foundation for Innovation (CFI), the Canadian Research Chairs Program (CRC), and the Research Granting Councils in fostering competition and enforcing a rigid ranking of "have and have-not" schools. What methods do educational institutions adopt to create research "teams," and how does this affect the education offered or the students who attend it?

Finally, how does this alter the relationship between universities and the public, and perhaps undermine the public interest where research decisions are concerned?

Fostering a climate of inter-institutional competition and therefore increasing the inequalities between institutions is also apparent in the area of fundraising. Drives for funding by the University of Toronto and McGill University, for example, are in no way matched by Trent University or the University of Manitoba, which have neither the number of alumni nor the lengthy history or reputation upon which to depend for promotion.[4] Furthermore, research funding from CFI, CRC, and the Granting Councils is often conditional on the educational institution finding "matching funds" from commercial/industrial sponsors. This requirement disadvantages many Canadian universities. As Tom Faulkner, president of the Dalhousie Faculty Association, has stated: "The CRC program clearly favours large 'full-service' universities over small colleges,... suggesting that public policy in Canada now seeks to foster a two-tiered university system."

Corporate funding

In the rush to become cost-effective, or—even better—*entrepreneurial*, institutions are looking for more ways to rely less on public money and more on private funds. This has ushered in a range of corporate sponsorships, exclusive marketing deals, or corporate research funding, which once again reinforces existing inequities between institutions, since some universities and colleges are better able to drum up corporate funding because of the size or wealth of their student body.

Furthermore, many of these exclusive marketing arrangements have unforeseen results. To give an example: According to the terms of the purchase agreement between the University of British Columbia and Coca-Cola, UBC is required to purchase 33.6 million cans or bottles of Coke over a 10-year period, ending in 2005 (UBC is set to receive almost $8.5 million over the duration of the contract). If this target is not met, Coke can extend the contract for two more years, during which the university would receive no additional funding ("UBC to Drink More Coke." *York Excalibur*. Sept. 5, 2001).

Universities and colleges are also being driven to cut costs. Institutions are relying more heavily on less expensive part-time instructors and sessionals, who do not have the benefits of tenure or many other basic worker rights. This affects the quality of education an institution offers—not because the instructors are necessarily less qualified, but because they do not have the protection of academic freedom, and this alters what is taught and sometimes the quality of the education students receive.

As well, it is much more difficult to perform at optimal levels when one's working conditions are tenuous.

What should be measured?

Quality is a critical component of higher education. After all, what good is a fully accessible university or college education if it is of inferior quality? *Missing Pieces* measures the provinces on quality, based on funding and its impact on students and faculty. It is precisely our definition of 'quality' that the Fraser Institute has taken issue with in its article, "Missing Pieces Misses the Goals of Advanced Education," (*Fraser Forum*, March 2001) by Hymie Rubenstein:

"[The] most troubling part of the CCPA's study is that its narrow range of indices involve mainly input variables that have no inherent relationship to academic outcomes. This is why the *MacLean's* ranking is far more credible. The magazine measures many more items, including input variables that are reasonably good proxies for high scholastic quality (incoming students' high school grades; the proportion of out-of-province students, the proportion of the budget devoted to the library; how many faculty win national awards and the proportion who are successful in securing federal government research grants). Maclean's also places a high emphasis on what many researchers consider to be the most important index of a university's stature, its reputation. (Why do so many outstanding students and faculty alike try to get into Harvard? Because it has such an outstanding reputation. Why does Harvard have such an outstanding reputation?

Because so many outstanding people try to get into Harvard. This is a tautology, but it works)."

It is significant that the Fraser Institute focuses on the concept of reputation as definitive in determining quality, precisely because once again it reduces education in general—and its quality in particular—to mere "measurable" outcomes. Why do the academic credentials of high school students determine the quality of the postsecondary institution that they attend? Would it not be more indicative of the quality of the school from which they just graduated? And why are high school marks a primary indicator (along with graduation rates after out-of-province students and timeliness of graduation[5]) of the worth of the student body?

According to *MacLean's*, "students are enriched by the input of their peers." (30) We agree. But to use as the primary determinant "the incoming students' average high school grades and the proportion of those with averages of 75% or higher" is, we suggest, limiting. Surely students from a wide range of backgrounds and experiences—cultural, geographical, social and economic—would be just as significant in determining student "input" in the quality of a PSE experience.

Rubenstein goes on to state that: "Factors such as actual learning outcomes, faculty research productivity, and overall institutional calibre are of little concern in the CCPA study because they have the unhappy effect of "reinforcing competition between individual institutions" and "have been used to vilify or promote institutions." Heaven forbid that universities should compete with each other for the brightest and best students, and that the results of this competition be made public!"
(http://www.fraserinstitute.ca/publications/forum/2001/03/section_13.html)

This suggests that the awards won by faculty and their degree of success in securing federal research grants are also significant indicators of institution quality. But it is a large assumption to make that it is only the quality research that gets money. Industry Canada has been very public in its push for innovation in education, specifically in the commercialization of research—it needn't be the quality or value inherent in the research itself that's important, so much as the *marketability* of the research.

Tautologies such as those used in the above quotation neatly avoid the discussions that need to take place when trying to determine the quality of PSE. Targeted research grant money is not, in and of itself, an indication of institutional quality. Federal or corporate money targeted to a specific individual or program may negatively impact the quality of education offered by the institution as a whole, as has been discussed by many researchers and elsewhere in *Missing Pieces*.

Rubenstein ignores considerations such as the type of research being undertaken, the implications and impacts of tying federal research money to private money, corporate funding of research, and the division of 'research faculty' from 'teaching faculty'. What is also ignored is the hierarchy that develops as teaching is potentially downplayed in stature because, after all, it is *research* that gets the grant money.

Factors such as learning outcomes are in fact very present in *Missing Pieces*, but in a broader context than Rubenstein addresses. If and how a student is able to complete and then use his or her education is a better measure of not just the province's commitment to making education affordable, but having those support mechanisms in place to allow graduates to pursue a career and to participate fully in society, unsaddled by debt or poverty.

Finally, the focus on "overall institutional calibre" is, we find, limiting and decontextualized. If reputation among alumni (as indicated by fundraising efforts) is indicative of the quality of an institution, then smaller, newer universities and colleges have little chance of developing a reputation based on the courses they offer, the quality of their instructors, or the accessibility and affordability of their programs. This definition of reputation is simply a measure of how clever the administration was in predicting the need to attract wealthy students before federal reductions in transfer payments or provincial cuts took place.

Such priorities further reinforce inequities between institutions and students—inequities that in large part already exist—and do nothing about increasing educational opportunity or accessibility for all students or institutions.

Missing Pieces does not compare individual institutions. It focuses on the provincial governments, the manner in which the agendas they set are reflected in their universities and colleges, and how students, faculty, support staff, researchers, and the public are (potentially and practically) affected.

The goals of *Missing Pieces* and other rankings, such as *MacLean's*, are not the same in this regard. We are, however, concerned with how ranking individual institutions according to criteria tied to a certain mindset and certain preconceptions does lead to a climate of competition based on flawed priorities.

This is not to say that we are inherently opposed to competition, as Rubenstein maintains. On the contrary: we would love to see institutions compete—not just for the "best and brightest," but for all students. This of course means that all universities and colleges need to ensure that their tuition fees are affordable so that all students can apply—regardless of the province in which they live or their level (or parental level) of income.

We would be thrilled if all institutions made public the relationships they were forging with the private sector, at what cost, to what effect—so that students, faculty, support staff, researchers, activists and citizens could address the issue of corporatization of research or the exclusive marketing arrangements directly, unfettered by secret boardroom meetings.

Universities and colleges that made the protection of academic freedom—particularly in light of the cases of Nancy Olivieri, David Healy and David Noble, among others—a fundamental priority, instead of bowing to the demands of private sector funders, would be thoroughly commended. We would applaud universities and colleges that refrain from treating international students as cash cows, and that control tuition fees rather than raise them to accumulate revenue at the expense of equity and accessibility.

Missing Pieces is not about avoiding comparisons. Rather, it is about determining where real comparisons need to be made: at the level of the decision-makers. This is about assessing provincial governments' education policies compared to those of other provinces. How much access do students have to faculty? How has lack of government funding contributed to the rise of corporate dollars and corporate influence in education? What is the state of academic freedom on university and college campuses? To what extent are governments committed to keeping tuition fees affordable and education accessible?

These are the comparisons Canadians need to know about in order to understand the status of higher education in this country, and their access to it.❖

Endnotes

[1] Much of the background research for this paper is from K. Foley's *Why Stop After High School?: A descriptive analysis of the most important reasons that high school graduates do not continue to PSE*, 2001 and COGEM Research Inc.'s *Qualitative Assessment of Non-attendees' Decision-Making and Attitudes Towards Post-secondary Education*, 2001. Both of these papers were prepared for the Millennium Scholarship Foundation.

[2] Comprehensive research includes loans by federal/provincial governments; parents, spouse and other relatives; private banks; cashing in RRSPs; and credit card debt.

[3] For example Women's Studies is not recognized as a discipline by the Social Sciences and Humanities Granting Council.

[4] Reputation is worth 20% in *MacLean's* rankings and is comprised of opinions from university officials, guidance counsellors, corporate recruiters, heads of organizations and CEOs. We suggest that this is likely a very accurate means of predicting which schools would have successful fundraising campaigns.

[5] Timeliness of graduation ("the percentage of full-time undergraduate students who go on to graduate within one year of the expected time period") is also a somewhat limiting indicator, especially since the timeliness of graduation is increasingly impacted by student finances and rising tuition fees, both of which are virtually impossible to predict.

Education and human capital
By John McMurtry

The university students I teach are the first children of the global market regime. They all have been conditioned to understand their education as a means to more money for themselves. *Cogito ergo sum* has become, *I am the money that can become more money by getting my degree.*

In this squalid market ethic, rising tuition fees are costs of investment in "human capital," while money capital is the meaning of life. Thus we see corporate globalization increasingly constructing the minds of the next generation as consumer and sales functions on the demand end, and obedient labour and service mechanisms on the supply end—all for stockholders to extract more money returns to themselves at the top of the feeding cycle. There is no remainder in the value system.

Corporate domination of society over recent decades has proven its danger to all forms of education. The quest for wider and deeper understanding by humanity's inherited codes of meaning has been systemically sacrificed to mindless market opportunism. In and out of the classroom, students are relentlessly indoctrinated to fit as temporary functions for global corporate money sequences. Their minds and bodies are cumulatively degraded in the process. In the world's leading market, the vocabulary of youth has been halved since commercial television came on line, obesity from corporate junk food has multiplied across age groups to over 40% of the population, and most find it difficult to comprehend more than a few sentences of prose at a time.[1]

Conditioned by the global market's system-selectors to be passive and predictable reactors to corporate stimuli flooding their environment with unconnected images and messages to "buy," the young have been dumbed down towards the lowest common denominator of mass appetite without thought. The telemarketing of unneeded commodities then replaces the vocation of serving others as the meaning of their graduation. Social learning is simultaneously foreclosed because there is no critical feedback loop in this self-referential value calculus. Turning money into more money for money investors is "the end of history."

Real value vs. money value

Neoclassical economics is at the heart of the problem because it can recognize *no* ground of value other than monetized capital, the God of all value. As with Yaheweh in the past, only in idolatrous form, any other source of value is the Enemy and to be abhorred. Yet if we consider the meaning of *capital* more carefully, we discover a home truth that has been lost for an era. Deriving its meaning from the original root of "cattle"— the wealth of milk, meat and energy that reproduces and grows into more if not consumed— "capital" has a deeper meaning than we suppose. At bottom, it means *life wealth that is used to produce more life wealth*.

Money capital, in contrast, is not really wealth or capital at all, but money control *of* wealth. What is fatefully missed by the premises of market culture is that money does not designate *value*, but only its possessor's *demand on* value. Money capital, in fact, never increases wealth, but only *claims on* wealth by those who control it. On the other hand, life capital is real capital. As the means of life that produce more means of life, it is the real basis of every breath we take and morsel we eat— what serves life as a means of life to become more comprehensive life. All value, in the end, is life value, and all real capital enables more life, not more money.

Life capital has two major forms: natural capital and human capital. Both are being increasingly degraded by money capital absolutism. The global market system cumulatively toxifies and strips social and ecological life-organization to multiply the money-demand of private stockholders, but no problem registers to this value calculus because it has no life coordinates.

Human capital in the undistorted sense is *sound education, what causes society's store and bearers of human knowledge to reproduce and grow*. No operation of the real economy can occur without the learned capabilities education produces and develops from one generation to the next. Yet within the closed box of *money capital*—money becoming more money for money possessors— neither human nor natural capital counts for any value except as each serves this hungry-ghost money sequence. The world of value is thus turned upside down. Means of life to produce more means of life otherwise in scarce supply, the true meaning of an *economy*, are used only to return more money to those who control money. In consequence, the Earth and the human species itself face the greatest crisis of economic misrule in history.

Seeing through money-capital fetishism

Canada's long-serving Minister of Finance recently declared to an environmental audience that natural and human capital—the primary forms of life capital—must be "protected," and went on to assert that this was all part of "a revolution in the structure of our economy in the mindset of our people."[2] So far, one might think Paul Martin got it right. But the words were hardly out of his mouth than he contradicted the meaning of what he said by adding that this "revolution" began with his halving of the government deficit-to-GDP ratio in the 1990s!

The contradiction is blatant. The deficit was paid down by Martin's reduction of health, education and social assistance transfers to provinces by $24 billion in one year, and by halving the environmental budget—even though these *investments in human and natural capital* accounted for only 6% of the deficit growth by a multi-refereed study of his own ministry. Martin's policies were, in fact, *a massive assault on human and natural capital* masquerading as "necessary for the economy." Meanwhile, public investment in human capital still remains completely excluded from public accounts as capital investment.

At the same time, the government of Canada is on a trade-deal binge to open all education budgets across the world to corporate for-profit management—over $2,000,000,000,000 in what DFAIT calls "procurement opportunities."[3] This is the secret meaning of NAFTA's "trade in services" and the WTO's GATS negotiations.

The key to every society's defence of educational heritage is to understand that "human capital" is *not* an ancillary function to serve money capital and corporate profit. No more fatal error could mislead humanity. *True human capital* is the opposite. It means *ever greater wealth of human life capabilities being built and passed from one generation to the next*. The global corporate market is bringing us the reverse: *ever more reckless depredation of life capital to enrich decoupled financial circuits.* Looted environments and hollowed education systems are the result. This is money capital in its carcinogenic stage.[4]

The life capital turn

The movement to understanding *capital* as more than the reified subsystem of money capital is centuries old. Jane Austen's male characters were typed as so many pounds per year, the heyday of money-fetish capital. But this problem is many times more destructive today. Other kinds of capital are finally being recognised—human, natural and social capital—but all remain subjugated to money capital. Do not underestimate the theocratic fundamentalism at work here.

Consider the National Science Organization Working Group which is now planning a country-wide research authority, a National Academy for Canada. It seems a fine idea. But the problem is that the administrative mover of the proposal is Dr. Tom Brzustowski, who is on record as saying as former Ontario Deputy Minister of Education: "I contend that the one global object of education must be to create wealth [sic]—to export products in which our knowledge and skills provide the value added, to develop new services which we can offer for trade in the world market."[5]

"Human capital" here is understood as investment of money into education so that students turn into producers of net higher money revenues for business markets. This "value adding" property qualifies the bearers of this sequence as "human capital" because they *too* are transformed into money sequences producing more money value for private investors than what their training costs. This is money-capital fetishism. On the basis of its upside-down logic, education is the middle term between money inputs and more money outputs. The "growth" of aggregate monetized outputs is its doctrine of salvation. But its profit has become the deficit of the Earth and its culture the inversion of education.

A cultural insanity continues only so long as it is unrecognized. If money capital is not used to create means of life, as it increasingly does not, it is *dead capital*. It is demand on life that consumes and predates it with no return. This is what we should learn from any education worthy of the name.❖

Endnotes

[1] These figures are drawn from Editorial, "Hog Nation", *Earth Island Journal*, Spring 2000, p. 23 and Harper's Index, *Harper's Magazine*, June 2000, p. 11.

[2] Paul Martin, "Protecting the Environment: A Fundamental Value", *Minister of Finance News Release*, Ottawa, May 25, 2001.

[3] Read any issue of *CanadExport* from Canada's Department of Foreign Affairs and International Trade and you will see that while the government publicly promises WTO and FTAA protection of public education, it is simultaneously evangelizing the benefits of these trade treaties for education-budget contracts for Canadian transnational corporations.

[4] See my *The Cancer Stage of Capitalism* (London: Pluto Press, 1999) for a systematic explanation of this pattern.

[5] Cited by Bill Graham, President's Column, *OCUFA Bulletin*, 6:15 (1989), 2-3.

Access to education and training
By Bob Baldwin

Education and training are a vital source of economic opportunity and security for individual workers, just as they are a source of growth and adaptability for the economy as a whole and the public and private entities that make it up. With this in mind, an overview of the extent to which Canadian adults participated in education and training during the 1990s may be instructive. This overview is offered from several perspectives: a) the extent to which all adults participated in all types of education and training; b) the extent to which all adults participated in job-related education and training; and c) the extent to which employed adults participated in "employer-supported" job-related education and training.

In addition, a brief look is taken at the extent of participation in apprenticeship programs, as well as enrolment and tuition fees in universities and colleges. Apprenticeship programs are an important method of preparing people for many skilled trades, and they represent an important training model. While the general importance of post-secondary education is widely acknowledged, it is worth adding that many working people in Canada look forward to the prospect of having their children attend post-secondary schools.

Overall, the decade of the 1990s was one in which the importance of education and training received large amounts of rhetorical attention. Education and training were regularly cited as the keys to future prosperity. Yet, for the most part, the 1990s was not a decade of progress in terms of the participation by adults in education and training. Public financial support for education and training declined and, with respect to post-secondary education, barriers to full participation by all members of society seem to have been recreated.

Data on adult education and training in the 1990s

The source of data for the following discussion is Statistics Canada's Adult Education and Training Surveys (AETS) of 1992, 1994 and 1998. Each survey asked respondents about their education and training activity in the previous year (i.e., 1991, 1993 and 1997). The fact that the last of these surveys was conducted in 1997 means that there is a lack of timeliness in the most recent survey. As should be clear from the remarks below on the political context, this is indeed unfortunate.

The dates of the surveys also means that the data do not arise from similar stages in the economic cycle (i.e., peaks, downswings, troughs or upswings). This should prompt caution in drawing conclusions about trends. Statistics Canada is currently planning another AETS for 2002. The results of this survey will help in determining whether some of the things of which one sees hints in the 1997 data represent emerging trends.

It should be noted explicitly, too, that there is an important issue with respect to access to education and training that cannot be answered by AETS data. That is the extent to which people of colour, Aboriginal people, and people with disabilities have access to training.

The political context

In looking at the data, it is worth recalling the remarkable ebb and flow in the political rhetoric that surrounded the issue of training in the 1990s. At the beginning of the 1990s, the federal government launched the "Labour Force Development Strategy." This entailed a substantial increase in federal financial support for training that was financed in large part by cuts to regular unemployment insurance benefits. At the same time, federal government spokespersons were critical of the limited investment in training by private employers and threatened them with a training tax if they did not increase their "voluntary" efforts.

By mid-decade, the training rhetoric had all but died. Budgets were being squeezed in the deficit reduction exercise, and UI money became virtually the only federal government money available for training. Then, in the wake of the Quebec sovereignty referendum in 1995, the federal government announced that it would devolve responsibility for training to the provinces. In a few short years, training had gone from being the solution to all of our problems to an unmentionable.

The impetus to act in the training area never died. It has re-emerged in the context of the federal government's interest in the "knowledge economy." It has been re-labelled as a "skills" or "learning" agenda. But, to anyone who does not have to resort to misleading labels, it is the traditional interest in education and training that is enjoying a rhetorical renaissance at the end of the 20th and beginning of the 21st century. (Notwithstanding the renewed interest in training and education, the Canadian Labour Congress (CLC) is very concerned about the cuts to federal training budgets and the dismantling of the training infrastructure. (With respect to spending cuts, see Table 3).

In the early 1990s, there was a substantial increase in total federal government funding for training: from $1.2 billion in 1990 to a high-water mark of $2.1 billion in 1993. But major spending cuts left the federal government spending only $441 million in 2000, roughly $1.6 billion less than it spent seven years earlier.

The federal dollars spent on training come from either the UI program or general government revenues. If the money comes from the UI program, it can only fund training for people currently on UI or, as of 1996, people who have been on UI for the last three years. By contrast, if the money comes from general government revenues, it can be spent on anyone, including the currently employed and new entrants or re-entrants to the labour force. In practice, the general government revenue spending was focused on new entrants and re-entrants, who are often the most vulnerable participants in the labour force (e.g., immigrants, mothers returning to work after periods of child-raising, Aboriginal people, people with disabilities, people on Social Assistance).

Against this background, it is striking that the federal spending from general government revenues was declining throughout the 1990s. On the other hand, spending on training under UI increased dramatically in the early 1990s—from $334 million in 1990 to $1.4 billion in 1993—as part of a supposed reorientation of the UI program. But, by the year 2000, UI spending on training was back down to $341 million.

Given the intense political rhetoric that has surrounded the training issue, one might have expected that the 1990s would be a period of dramatic change in rates of participation in adult education and training. This expectation is not borne out by the numbers—at least not through to 1997.

Who participated in education and training

Table 1 shows for 1991, 1993 and 1997, the percentage of: all adults who participated in any form of education and training; the percentage of all adults who participated in job-related education and training; and all employed people who participated in

Table 1
Participation in adult education and training, by gender
Canada, 1991, 1993 and 1997

		1991	1993	1997
All types/all adults				
	Female	29.7	31.0	28.7
	Male	28.0	29.5	26.8
	Total	28.9	30.3	27.7
Job-related/all adults				
	Female	20.9	21.2	20.6
	Male	24.1	23.9	21.6
	Total	22.5	22.5	21.1
Employer supported, job-related/employed people				
	Female	23.5	23.8	24.3
	Male	25.3	24.0	22.7
	Total	24.5	23.9	23.4

Source: AETS

"employer- supported" job-related education and training.

In looking at the data in Table 1, four things merit comment:
1. There are no "dramatic" changes in any of the numbers during the 1990s; but
2. overall, the percentage of adults participating in education and training is somewhat lower in 1997 than 1993;
3. female participation in "employer-supported," job-related education and training surpassed male participation during the 1990s; and
4. less than one in four employed workers received any support at all from their employers to get job-related education and training.

The last three comments need some elaboration.

It is probably too early to say whether the decline in participation in education and training by adults is permanent and/or linked to federal spending cuts. The results of the 2002 AETS will be helpful in assessing these issues.

Table 2 may provide some circumstantial evidence that federal funding cuts have led to lower participation of adults in education and training. That table shows a relatively significant decline in participation in job-related education and training for people not in the labour force. Bearing in mind the previous discussion of whose training is financed by UI vs general government revenues, it is people not in the labour force who are most likely to be adversely affected by the decline in funding for training financed by general government revenues.

The fact that employed women were more likely than employed men to participate in "employer-supported" education and training by the end of the 1990s is an important development. However, this development did not occur uniformly across all occupations and income levels.

In terms of broad occupational categories, women were more likely than men to participate in employer-supported education and training if they worked in the professional and managerial category. In 1997, 35.4% of women in this broadly-defined category participated in employer-supported education and training vs 32.1% of men. But they were slightly less likely than men to participate in em-

Table 2
Percentage of the adult population
participating in job-related training by labour force status
Canada, 1991, 1993 and 1997

	1991	1993	1997
In labour force	30.3	30.0	28.6
Employed	31.7	31.4	29.4
Unemployed	18.7	19.7	20.4
Not in labour force	6.7	7.5	6.1
Total	22.5	22.5	21.1

Source: AETS

Table 3
Government of Canada training expenditures by source
1990, 1993 and 2000
($ millions)

	General government revenues	Unemployment Insurance	Total
1990	918	334	1252
1993	611	1475	2086
1996	395	1,152	1942
2000	100	341	441

Source: HRDC: Statistics Bulletin (FAS Policy and Systems) / CLFDB Documents

ployer-supported education and training if they were in clerical sales and service occupations (18.1% vs 20.0%). Women were much less likely than men to participate in employer-supported education and training if they were in "labour-intensive" or "blue collar" occupations (8.9% vs 17.0%).

Moreover, while women were more likely than men to receive more employer-supported education and training over a wide income spectrum, this generalization did not hold true for women with incomes below $15,000. Indeed, in the income range below $15,000, rates of participation in employer-supported education and training were low and roughly equal for men and women at about 10%.

It is possible that the 2002 AETS will not support the conclusion that employed women are more likely to participate in employer-supported training than employed men. However, this development does seem to be part of a multi-dimensional and long-evolving process of relative improvement in the position of women in the labour force.

Finally, it is important to note that the low level of employer-supported training may actually flatter the actual efforts that employers are making. Employer support is defined very broadly in the AETS and encompasses minimal employer effort.

Over the years, one of the common conclusions reached by researchers looking at employer-supported training is that it tends to reinforce privilege or existing advantage in the labour market. In other words, employer-supported education and training is more likely to be provided to people who were already advantaged in terms of their education, income and occupational status, and gender. Except for the longstanding male advantage just discussed, the AETS data tend to confirm this general relationship through the 1990s. They also confirm the greater likelihood of people getting employer-supported education and training if they work for large vs small companies. Because these relationships remained quite stable through the 1990s—again with the gender exception noted above—they will not be pursued here.

It is important to note that, while employer-supported education and training clearly supports the prevailing sources of advantage, it does not necessarily follow that it does so to a greater degree than other parts of the training and education system for adults. One quick and partial observation will serve to illustrate the point.

The data in Tables 4 and 5 provide interesting evidence on this point. On the one hand, they clearly show that, as one moves up the occupational hierarchy, employees are more like to get employer-supported job-related training. Thus, in 1997, 23.4% of all professional and managerial employees got employer-supported job-related training compared to 15.6% of blue collar employees. But employer-supported job-related training accounted for only 57% of job-related training for professional and managerial employee,s whereas it accounted for 79% of all training for blue collar workers. This suggests that the job-related training that was not provided by employers was even more unevenly distributed than that provided by employers.

What is clear in Table 4 is that, while employer-supported training reinforces advantage among occupational groups, it does so to a lesser degree than "the total system" of job-related education and training. Without further investigation, this result should not be generalized to all aspects of employer-supported training, but it illustrates the general point that this type of analysis is needed. It is, by the way,

Table 4
Employer supported job-related training as a percentage of all job-related training by major occupational group
Canada, 1991, 1993 and 1997

	1991	1993	1997
White collar: professional/managerial	53	54	57
White collar: ?	68	66	76
Labour intensive/blue collar	81	76	79

Source: AETS

Table 5
Percentage of the population participating in job-related training, and in employer supported job-related training by major occupational group
Canada, 1991, 1993 and 1997

	1991	1993	1997
White collar: professional/managerial			
All employed	46.1	43.8	40.9
Employer-supported	24.5	23.7	23.4
White collar: ?			
All employed	26.8	26.6	25.0
Employer-supported	18.1	17.6	18.9
Labour intensive/blue collar			
All employed	21.2	21.8	19.8
Employer-supported	17.2	16.6	15.6

Source: AETS

Table 6
Mean annual number of hours spent on job-related training per employee participant by employer-sponsored and non-employer sponsored training
Canada, 1991, 1993 and 1997

	1991	1993	1997
Employer sponsored	71	76	92
Non-employer sponsored	219	246	354
Total	118	126	158

Source: AETS

Table 7
Registered apprentices

1991	1992	1993	1994	1995	1996	1997	1998
192,946	180,963	168,983	165,668	164,569	166,489	172,343	177,741

Source: Statistics Canada

a conclusion that is compatible with the CLC's view that an organizational framework that provides relevant information and support is necessary to make training and education effective for many people.

One clear trend in adult education and training in the 1990s was an increase in hours of education and training per year, per participant. This increase was found in all education and training and job-related education and training. Table 6 provides relevant data for job-related training broken down by employer-supported and non-employer-supported training. The increase in the total number of hours of education and training per participant is striking. So is the fact that the number of hours of non-employer-supported training is so much larger in absolute terms, and grew faster during the 1990s.

Apprenticeship trends in the 1990s

Within the realm of job-related adult education and training, apprenticeship has a special place for many working people. Unfortunately, as can be seen in Table 7, the first half of the 1990s was a period of declining participation in apprenticeship programs. There was a recovery in the number of apprentices in the latter half of the 1990s, but in 1998, the last year for which we have data, there were 15,000 fewer apprentices than in 1991.

Underlying the general decline in participation in apprenticeship were some significant variations among the trades. As can be seen in Table 8, the building construction trades had a decline of more than 12,000 apprentices and the electrical, electronics and related trades had a decline of nearly 8,000 apprentices. On the other hand, apprentices in the food and service areas increased by nearly 8,000.

The declining number of apprentices in the 1990s is important, in and of itself, as it is indicative of closing the pathway to what are typically good jobs. But in the case of the building trades there is added significance to the

Table 8
Registered apprenticeship training by industry

	1991	1997	1998
Building, construction trades	46,925	33,754	34,673
Electrical, electronics and related	37,035	28,384	29,065
Food and service	11,422	17,961	18,088
Industrial and mechanical trades	15,112	14,336	14,617
Metal fabricating trades	39,534	36,026	38,262
Motor vehicle and heavy equipment	39,316	38,002	38,658
Other trades	3,602	3,880	4,378
Total	192,946	172,343	177,741

Source: Statistics Canada

Table 9
Enrollment at Canadian universities and colleges
1990-1991 to 1998-1999

	University Full-Time	University Part-Time	University Total	College Full-Time	College Part-Time	College Total	University + College Total
1990-91	532,131	309,197	841,328	324,529	124,581	449,110	1,290,438
1991-92	553,953	313,326	867,281	349,207	140,604	489,811	1,357,092
1992-93	569,480	316,165	885,645	364,696	103,597	468,293	1,353,938
1993-94	574,320	300,284	874,604	369,192	98,430	467,622	1,342,226
1994-95	575,713	283,257	858,970	379,961	90,810	470,771	1,329,741
1995-96	573,194	273,215	846,409	391,282	87,689	478,971	1,325,380
1996-97	573,635	256,133	829,768	397,308	87,081	484,389	1,314,157
1997-98	573,099	249,673	822,772	398,643	91,577	490,220	1,312,992
1998-99	580,376	245,985	826,361	403,516	91,439	494,955	1,321,316

Source: Statistics Canada

declining participation in apprenticeship.

The construction workforce is currently an older workforce than is found in many other industries. Unless there is a significant increase in the number of new journeypersons in the years ahead, there is likely to be a serious skills shortage in the construction sector.

Post-secondary education

Total enrolment in post-secondary institutions was stable through the 1990s. As can be seen in Table 9, total enrolment in 1998-99 was 1,321,316, compared to 1,290,438 in 1990-91. This stability reflects a slight decline in university enrolment, from 841,328 to 826,316, which was more than offset by a 10% increase in college enrolment, from 449,110 to 494,955.

Within both universities and colleges, there was a substantial shift from part-time to full-time enrolment. Full-time enrolment increased as a share of total university enrolment, from 63% in 1990-91 to 70% in 1998-99. The same trend took place in the colleges, where full-time enrolment increased as a share of the total, from 72% to 82%, between 1990-91 to 1998-99. In context, it is worth noting that, while total university enrolment declined slightly, there was an increase in full-time enrolment at universities of nearly 50,000.

While total enrolment stayed strong in the 1990s, enrolment is being put at risk by the hefty increases in tuition fees across the country. As can be seen in Table 10, average annual tuition fees for undergraduate university students have more than doubled during the 1990s, from $1,464 in 1990-91 to $3,405 in 2000-2001. Over the entire decade of the 1990s, consumer prices increased by only 1.6%. In Table 11, we can also see that tuition fees have doubled their share as a source of university revenues, from roughly 11% at the beginning of the decade to roughly 20% at the end of the decade.

Major hikes in tuition fees are recreating the barriers to education that were reduced substantially in the late 1960s and 1970s. They not only jeopardize total enrolments, but they create financial burdens which are felt most heavily by families with moderate and low incomes. They clearly create the risk that post-secondary education will be available only to the wealthy, and this possible development will have adverse economic as well as social effects.❖

Table 10
Weighted average domestic undergraduate tuition fees
for Canada by province 1990-2001

	NF	PE	NS	NB	QC	ON	MB	SK	AB	BC	Canada
90-91	1344	1874	1941	1925	904	1680	1512	1545	1286	1808	1464
91-92	1544	2141	2232	2046	1311	1818	1848	1859	1544	1970	1706
92-93	1700	2298	2446	2265	1458	1942	2160	2129	1831	2128	1872
93-94	2000	2509	2701	2385	1550	2076	2272	2341	2209	2240	2023
94-95	2150	2647	2972	2390	1702	2283	2391	2543	2478	2434	2214
95-96	2312	2849	3246	2530	1702	2513	2510	2677	2745	2557	2371
96-97	2829	2950	3590	2781	1600	2981	2689	2727	2990	2592	2601
97-98	3216	3162	3890	3026	1803	3298	2907	3074	3239	2519	2864
98-99	3213	3328	4072	3217	1801	3648	3117	3263	3512	2519	3061
99-00	3370	3501	4278	3344	1832	4066	3452	3384	3722	2529	3292
00-01	3374	3499	4669	3585	1855	4219	3273	3676	3914	2511	3405

Source: Tabulations Prepared by the Centre for Education Statistics

Table 11
Student fees as a percentage of total university revenue
Canada, 1989 - 1999

Year	Student Fees
1989-90	11.19
1990-91	11.89
1991-92	12.99
1992-93	14.05
1993-94	15.04
1994-95	16.00
1995-96	16.87
1996-97	18.64
1997-98	19.53
1998-99	20.30

Source: Tabulations Prepared by the Centre for Education Statistics

Increasing the burden:
Student financial assistance in Canada

By Michael Conlon and Pam Frache

A response to Ross Finnie, Adjunct Professor, School of Policy Studies at Queen's University, "Measuring the Load, Easing the Burden: Canada's Student Loan Programs and the Revitalization of Canadian Post-secondary Education" in Commentary, No. 155, November 2001.

"Student loan schemes exist in more than 60 countries, making them an increasingly important financing mechanism for higher education."
—*Jamil Salmi, Education Manager, Latin American and the Caribbean Region, World Bank*[1]

"[A]n enhanced loan-relief system could also provide students with the means to shoulder higher costs for their post-secondary education."
—*Ross Finnie, Adjunct Professor in the School of Policy Studies at Queen's University*[2]

In the November 2001 issue of the C.D. Howe Institute's *Commentary*, Ross Finnie presents a series of recommendations for changing the Canada Student Loan Program and increasing tuition fees. Given the profound implications associated with implementing these proposals, it is worth responding to the paper in some detail.

To begin, it is important to understand the starting point of Finnie's analysis. Although not explicitly stated, the title of the article offers a telling sign: "Measuring the Load, Easing the Burden: Canada's Student Loan Programs and the Revitalization of Canadian Post-secondary Education." It is clear from the title of the document that the underlying basis for suggesting changes to the Canada Student Loan Program is not the revitalization of student financial assistance, but rather the revitalization of post-secondary education through the imposition of higher tuition fees.

This response paper will argue that Finnie's document is little more than a thinly veiled effort to make palatable the downloading of post-secondary education costs onto students and their families. Under Finnie's model, the restructuring of student financial assistance is presented solely as a means to justify further tuition fee increases.

The underlying theme of Finnie's paper is that post-secondary education has been underfunded for the past dozen years, and Finnie is rightly critical of this fact. He notes, for example, that, while government contributions to higher education have declined, tuition fees have not adequately offset these decreases in funding.[3] However, this contention reveals that Finnie embraces the idea that tuition fees should compensate for inadequate government funding. He notes that tuition fees "only cover a relatively small portion—somewhere around a third—of the full costs of [post-secondary education]".[4] As a solution, Finnie is proposing a scheme designed to generate support for tuition fee hikes, despite the fact that the vast majority of Canadians do not want to see tuition fees increase, but rather want to see an accessible system of higher education.[5]

It should be noted that Finnie's arguments mirror those of William Leggett, Principal of Queen's University, where Finnie is Adjunct Professor in the School of Policy Studies. Leggett and other university presidents argue that declining quality means that tuition fees must increase, and therefore debt levels should be expanded to accommodate such increases.[6]

Finnie's arguments also portray a profound pessimism and politically motivated fatalism about the possibility of convincing provincial and federal governments to adequately invest in higher education. This pessimism provides Finnie with a political alibi for his superficial solution that the only way to address government underfunding is by increasing tuition fees. He notes that his scheme would be a "means of raising some desperately needed new funds by making viable additional payments on the part of students, along with contributions from both the provincial and federal levels of government—an option that would be much more problematic without the sorts of reforms suggested here." Although most of these issues are raised at the conclusion of his paper, it is important to bring them to light at the beginning of any critique, since this highly political perspective is the key feature of the reforms he has presented.

Despite the cynicism of Finnie and those who advocate similar views, there is a vibrant and mobilized political movement fighting for progressive solutions to government underfunding. Where students and faculty have been united, it has been possible to lobby governments to increase their commitment to accessible higher education. Over the previous two years, five provincial governments have shown leadership by freezing or reducing tuition fees. Moreover, such policy measures have proven extremely popular within the voting populace.

In Ontario, the government has failed to take steps to regulate access and has moved further away from such policies by allowing unlimited tuition fee increases for certain programs. The resulting increases have been particularly stark for college level programs like dental hygiene where tuition fees have increased by between 300% and 400% in only three years. Medical school tuition fees at the University of Toronto have increased from $4,850 in 1997-98 to $14,700 for the current year. Small wonder then, as demonstrated by public opinion surveys over the past two years, that more than 80% of those surveyed support a freeze or reduction in tuition fees.

Opposition to tuition fee increases is based on the very real fear experienced by working people that the costs of post-secondary education are becoming beyond their economic reach.[7] What is crucial to note about Finnie is that his work provides a convenient excuse for the provincial and federal governments to ignore calls for more public funding for an accessible post-secondary system. Regrettably, this lazy way of doing politics has extended to many college and university presidents, who now define their government relations strategy by begging the government to allow them to charge higher tuition fees.

There can be no doubt that one reason for the heightened level of concern about increasing tuition fees and student debt is the ongoing campaign launched by the Canadian Federation of Students. Since before the 1990s decade, the Federation has been highlighting the impact of rising tuition fees and the chronic underfunding of colleges and universities in Canada. As a result of the Federation's campaign, tuition fees were frozen by the British Columbia government in the mid-1990s and remained frozen until this year, when tuition fees were reduced by 5%.

In the fall of 1994, the federal government introduced the single largest cut to social programme spending—including post-secondary education—under the auspices of the Canada Health and Social Transfer (CHST). At that time, Human Resources and Development Canada also proposed to revamp the Canada Student Loan Program by introducing an "income-contingent loan repayment" scheme. The book *Double-Vision: The Inside Story of the Liberals in Power* by Edward Greenspon and Anthony Wilson-Smith highlights the impact of the Canadian Federation of Students in galvanizing opposition to a loan repayment scheme that would allow tuition fees to increase. As stated in *Double-Vision,* it was through the Federation's mobilizing campaign that "Axworthy had lost control of the critical terms of the debate."[8] More recently, at a January 23, 2002 meeting in Vancouver, keynote speaker and former Minister of HRDC, Lloyd Axworthy, publicly credited the Canadian Federation of Students with forcing the federal government to retreat on its regressive income-contingent loan repayment scheme.[9]

The fact that the federal government was proposing the ICR scheme at the same time as it was cutting $1 billion from social prograe spending—more than a third of the HRDC budget—was no accident. As has been well documented by the Canadian Federation of Students in the early 1990s, the mid-1990s, and again last year, ICR schemes were developed as a mechanism to enable federal and provincial governments to download the costs of higher education onto students and their families. In other jurisdictions where ICR schemes have been introduced, tuition fees have increased dramatically.[10] Nowhere in his paper does

Finnie address the issue of the effect that higher tuition fees and higher student debt have on access to post-secondary education. Like most of those who advocate private solutions to the growing crisis in public post-secondary education, Finnie ignores the social consequences of his policy suggestions.

Finnie's private solutions to Canada's post-secondary education system should be placed in an international context. The World Bank echoes many of Finnie's suggestions in a document entitled: *Development in Practice, Higher Education: The Lessons of Experience*, published in 1994.[11] The Bank devotes an entire chapter to the issue of "Diversifying the Funding of Public Institutions and Introducing Incentives for Their Performance." In this section, the Bank has the following to say:

> "The financial base of public higher education can be strengthened by mobilizing a greater share of the necessary financing from students themselves... Cost-sharing can be pursued by charging tuition fees in public institutions and eliminating subsidies for non-instructional costs. Governments can permit public institutions to establish their own tuition fees without interference."[12]

It is also no surprise that in this same chapter, "Diversifying the Funding of Public Institutions," the Bank reveals its vision for student financial assistance, advocating for income-contingent loan repayment schemes. Under this kind of scheme, students would be allowed—and encouraged—to borrow as much as required to purchase their education. This would ensure that students' borrowing capacity keeps up with tuition fees, allowing for the privatization of higher education funding. Upon graduation, students would then repay their loans based on post-graduation income. While on the surface this may sound equitable, the scheme essentially condemns students to lifetimes of debt—especially those who will earn relatively less.

In countries like New Zealand where this kind of scheme has been introduced, it is estimated that student debt now exceeds the country's national debt at $4.1 billion dollars.[13] Moreover, by the year 2005 it is estimated that student debt will exceed $15 billion. The student debt crisis has exacerbated that country's "brain-drain," with many high-debtor graduates working abroad where wages are higher so that they may repay their debts more quickly.[14] For those in less lucrative employment, student debt has prevented many from being able to participate in the economy, being saddled with debts the size of mortgages—but without the houses to show for it.

In his document, Finnie underlines the impact that government funding cuts have had on the higher education system in Ontario, yet he argues that, if students were to pay more of the costs, then governments themselves might be more inclined to help with funding. Of course, this logic is contrary to the lived experience of Ontario institutions. In Ontario, the largest funding cuts have corresponded with the highest increases in tuition fees. At the same time, per capita funding for post-secondary education in Ontario is among the lowest of all jurisdictions in North America. In addition, there is an extreme faculty shortage, and student-teacher ratios have soared.

As a strong advocate of private funding for higher education, the World Bank makes the case for governments to create incentives for corporations to make financial donations to post-secondary education. In this regard, the Bank highlights India as the developing country with the most "generous" tax incentives: 150% of donations are tax deductible. In other words, for every dollar donated to a post-secondary institution, the corporation will receive $1.50 in tax breaks from the government (*Development*, p. 43). Finally, the Bank argues that an important income-generating activity for governments would be the introduction of "government matching funds linked to outside income in some ratio or the inclusion of income generated from outside sources as a positive element in funding formulas" (*Development*, pp. 41-42). This proposal is nothing short of a transfer of public dollars to private corporations.

It is clear that the models advocated by the World Bank do not favour publicly-funded higher education. The Bank proposes complicated formulas to encourage governments to abdicate their responsibility to fund post-secondary education adequately. As a figleaf for enabling governments to withdraw from education funding, the World Bank—and indeed, Finnie himself—favours the concept of "targeted-funding" for student financial assistance. The idea sounds harmless on the surface: those who can afford to pay for their education should, while those who cannot will have debt loads reduced or forgiven. However, this model fails to recognize that many students from middle and lower income backgrounds may simply choose to avoid the risky venture of saddling themselves with excessive debt. These are the students who will not be captured in any student loan scheme that relies in the first instance on amassing high debt levels, with the possibility that some of that debt may be eliminated.

And while there is not a shred of evidence to suggest that increasing tuition fees, regardless of the student financial assistance model in place, will enhance access to higher education, there is growing evidence that increasing tuition fees in Canada and elsewhere have compromised access. Statistics Canada has presented data demonstrating a widening gap in higher education participation rates between students from affluent backgrounds and those from middle and lower income backgrounds.[15] This trend corresponds to a period of dramatic increases in tuition fees across the country. Moreover, studies at the universities of Guelph, Waterloo and Western Ontario have all documented the changing socio-economic composition of students in different medical class cohorts.[16]

In his paper, Finnie argues that the student debt crisis has been exaggerated. However, average debt upon graduation is $25,000—a figure released by Human Resources Development Canada in 1998. Neither this figure nor the figures presented by Finnie reflect actual student debt. For example, according to research recently released by the Millennium Scholarship Foundation, average credit card debt incurred by graduating students is $1,500.[17] Far from representing students' joy of borrowing as suggested by Finnie, it is a sad statement indeed that students are funding their education at interest rates 300% higher than standard lending rates. That those who are able to access this source of debt do so is not reflective of students' willingness to choose increased debt. Instead, it reflects the fact that students are increasingly held hostage by the very real fear of losing access to post-secondary education. We can only speculate about the number of students who are lost to the system because they do not have the financial confidence to incur debt.

Moreover, governments have implemented stricter borrowing criteria to determine a student's eligibility for student loans. This in itself has made higher education out of reach for those whose backgrounds require a more heavy, and perhaps unstable, reliance on credit. These are the people most in need of accessible higher education. These are also the people for whom the door has closed on their educational aspirations.

Although Finnie recognizes the problems associated with stricter borrowing criteria, he makes an incredible leap in logic to assert that students would be "glad" to incur higher debts were they given the opportunity. In other words, he argues, tuition fees should be allowed to rise, students should be allowed to borrow more with fewer restrictions, and they will be pleased to do so in exchange for higher quality education. This position has been advocated at one time or another by both the former Reform Party of Canada and the Ontario Undergraduate Student Association.[18]

There is simply no basis for asserting that higher tuition fees translate into higher quality education, as Ontario's experience with private colleges demonstrates. Moreover, the consequences of burdening an entire generation with excessive debt have been well-documented in Australia and New Zealand. Student debt has skyrocketed, tuition fees have put higher education out of the reach of ordinary citizens, and governments have abdicated their responsibilities to fund public education. When Finnie's report is stripped of its academic veneer, this is his vision for post-secondary reform in Canada.

Even where the World Bank has been successful in determining government policy, the conditions for post-secondary education have not improved. Indeed, in a document outlining the global challenges facing systems of higher education, Philip Altbach and Todd Davis have stated the dilemma explicitly:

Demands for access come into conflict with another of the flashpoints of controversy of the present era—funding. Higher education is an expensive undertaking, and there is much debate concerning how to fund expanding academic systems. Current approaches to higher education funding emphasize the need for "users" to pay for the cost of instruction, as policy-makers increasingly view higher education as something that benefits the individual, rather than as a "public good" where the benefits accrue to society. This new thinking, combined with constrictions on public expenditures in many countries, have meant severe financial problems for academe.

Academic systems and institutions have tried to deal with these financial constraints in several ways. Loan programs, the privatization of some public institutions, and higher tuition are among the alternatives to direct government expenditure. In many parts of the world, including most of the major industrialized nations, conditions of study have deteriorated in response to financial constraints. Enrolments have risen, but resources, including faculty, have not kept up with needs. Academic infrastructures, including libraries and laboratories, have been starved of funds. Less is spent on basic research. Conditions of study have deteriorated in many of the world's best-developed academic systems, including Germany and France. Students have taken to the streets in large numbers to protest declining budgets and poor conditions for the first time since the 1960s.[19]

The present dilemma for Canada is whether our federal and provincial governments are prepared to invest in higher education to ensure that it remains excellent *and* accessible. The outcome of the debate in Ontario and throughout Canada is critical, since this debate is well underway internationally. Are students prepared to accept the intransigence of governments and the World Bank, who are advocating the state's retreat from ensuring that every qualified student has access to the education so critical for economic survival? The response in Canada and around the world would suggest that they are not.

Finnie's vision of "improving" student financial assistance is simply opening the door to increases in tuition fees that will put education out of the reach of ordinary Canadians. It is premised on the assumption that government cannot be convinced to change their spending priorities. That academics and administrators alike have been thoroughly imbued with such pessimism in our democratic institutions that they have abandoned the arena altogether reflects poorly on the health of democracy in Canada. Yet, in contradiction to such views, where public support has been galvanized, where decision-makers have had the courage to put the needs and desires of its own constituents ahead of the corporate agenda, significant improvements have been achieved in many social spheres.

The Canadian Federation of Students—along with the vast majority of Canadians—remains committed to a post-secondary education system that is of high quality and accessible to all. We call on all those who support a publicly-funded, accessible system of higher education to oppose any schemes that will further erode the affordability of higher education.❖

Endnotes

1. Salmi, Jamil. 2001. *Student Loans: The World Bank Experience*. International Higher Education, Winter 2001. p.1.
2. Finnie, Ross. 2001. *Measuring the Load, Easing the Burden, Canada's Student Loan Programs and the Revitalization of Canadian Postsecondary Education*. C.D. Howe Institute Commentary. p 22.
3. Ibid. p. 26.
4. Ibid. p. 30.
5. In three independent surveys over two years, 82% of those surveyed opposed increasing tuition fees. See Feedback Research Corporation poll, *GTA Survey*, September 2001 (for poll results and tables, see the web site of the Ontario Confederation of University Faculty Associations at www.ocufa.on.ca). Also see the Ipsos-Reid poll, *Ontarians and Access to Post Secondary Education*, April 2001 (for poll results and tables, see the OCUFA web site at www.ocufa.on.ca). Finally, also see the Angus Reid poll, *Ontarians to Harris—Hold the Line on Tuition Fees*, February 2000.
6. In 1998, the Ontario government introduced a policy to allow for the complete deregulation of all graduate programmes, as well as certain professional and post-diploma programmes, resulting in tuition fee increases significantly greater than the rate of inflation and increased earnings.
7. According to the Canadian Association of University Teachers, access to higher education is linked to family circumstances. Research by CAUT shows that in 1990-91, 20% of the lowest income families would have had to set aside 14% of their after-tax earnings to pay the cost of one family member to attend university. By 1998-99, those same families would have had to set aside 23% of their after-tax income to allow one family member to attend university. By contrast, the top fifth of high-income families would have seen the amount of after-tax income required for university shift from 3% to 4% (CAUT, *Education Review*, Vol. 3, No. 2).
8. Greenspon, Edward and Anthony Wilson-Smith. 1997 *Double-Vision: The Inside Story of the Liberals in Power*, Seal Edition, Doubleday Canada Limited: Toronto. p. 192-193.
9. Graduate Student Leadership Conference, University of British Columbia, Keynote Address, Hon. Lloyd Axworthy, January 23-26, 2002.
10. See various papers at Center for International Higher Education, Boston College, available online at: <http://www.bc.edu/bc_org/avp/soe/cihe/Center.html>.
11. World Bank. 1994. *Development in Practice, Higher Education: The Lessons of Experience*, Washington: International Bank for Reconstruction and Development.
12. Ibid, p. 41.
13. Australian Union of Students, Tertiary Update, Vol. 4, No. 44, December 13, 2001.
14. Australian Union of Students, Tertiary Update, Vol. 4, No. 29, August 13, 2001. It is also noted that "[a] survey of dentistry students at Otago University has found that less than half of the graduates are remaining in the country, with the rest flocking overseas to earn higher salaries and pay off debts of between $50,000 and $100,000. The Dental Council's 'Workforce Analysis' report shows that only 23 of 54 dentistry students graduating in 1996 were still in the coun-

try last year. According to the figures, retention rates four years after graduation are at about 43% compared with rates in earlier years of 50% to 70%." Student representatives say they hope new government funding, which has halved the cost of dentistry tuition, may mean more students remain in New Zealand after they graduate.

15 Statistics Canada. 2001. *Participation in Postsecondary Education and Family Income*. The Daily, Friday, December 7. Available online at: <http://www.statcan.ca/Daily/English/011207/d011207c.htm>.

16 Medical Students of the University of Western Ontario. 2001. *Access to Medical Education: A Proposal to the University of Western Ontario Senate*, Sid Gilbert, Ian McMillan, Linda Quirke, and Joanne Duncan-Robinson. "Accessibility and Affordability of University Education," University of Guelph, December, 1999. University of Waterloo Federation of Students, *The Changing Face of Ontario Universities: Are Universities Becoming the Domain of the Rich?*, 1998.

17 Canada Millennium Scholarship Foundation. 2002. *Student Financial Survey – Baseline Results*. Canada Millennium Scholarship Foundation Research Series: Montreal.

18 See Parliament of Canada, Hansard, Monday, December 5, 1994 - Private Members' Business, <http://collection.nlc-bnc.ca/>.

19 Altbach, Philip G. and Todd M. Davis. 1999. *Global Challenge and National Response: Notes for an International Dialogue on Higher Education*. International Higher Education, Winter.

Audit:
Trent University
By Liz Blackwell

Board of Governors

Reps
Chair Gary E. Wolff, B.A., M.B.A., F.C.A. **Vice-Chair** Jane C. Dudas Daryl Bennett Paul Crookall, B.Sc., M.B.A., Ph.D. Richard Dicerni, B.A. M.P.A. Marie Doyle Glen Easson David Glassco, B.A., M.A., Ph.D. Peter Gzowski C.C., LL.D., D.LITT. Michael Izzo Richard Krug B.Comm. Ana P. Lopes B.A. Jordan Lyall Lynn McDonald, B.A. Barbara J. McGregor, B.A., LL.B. Reid Morden, B.A. Bonnie M. Patterson, M.A., M.L.S. Cecil A. Rabinovitch, B.A. Kate Ramsay, B.A. Gary T. Reker, B.A., M.A.Sc., Ph.D. William J. Saunderson D.U., F.C.A. Larry E. Seeley, B.A.SC., M.A.SC., PH.D. Edward W.H. Tremain, B.A., F.C.A. Len Vernon, B.SC.,C.A. Douglas Young, H.B.A.

Official Senate visitors to the Board of Governors for 2001-2002
Jacqueline Solway (Faculty) Pieter Funnekotter (Student)

Honorary Members
Thomas J. Bata, C.C. Jalynn H. Bennett, B.A. Erica Cherney, B.COM. John D. de Pencier Sylva M. Gelber, O.C., LL.D., D.HUM.L. Merritt E. Gordon, B.A.SC., P.ENG. Jon K. Grant, B.A., LL.D. John G. McCarney, B.A., Q.C. Mary A. Mogford, B.A. David T.C. Moore, B.A., LL.D. Keith C. Pilley, B.COM. Robert W.F. Stephenson, M.A.. LL.B. James A. Swanston, B.A. Helen M. Whiteside, B.A. Judith R. Wilder, B.A. Tod Willcox, B.SC., P.ENG.

Corporate Interests on BoG
Daryl Bennett is President of the Liftlock Group of Companies.

Richard Dicerni is Executive Vice President and Corporate Secretary of Ontario Power Generation where he is responsible for the stewardship of the environmental portfolio, public affairs, government relations, including OPG's relationship with the Canadian Nuclear Safety Commission.

Lynn McDonald is Managing Director, Canadian Credit Capital Markets for CIBC World Markets in Toronto.

Larry Seeley is President and Chief Executive Officer of Lakefield Research Limited.

Doug Young is President and CEO of Cygnal Technologies Corporation based in Oshawa.

Corporate Partners
Aramark
Zoom
Bell

Funding Breakdown
*for year 2000

Provincial grants: $22.3 million (52.1%)
Student tuition fees: $19.1 million (44.6%)
Donations and grants: $0.8 million (1.9%)
Miscellaneous: $0.6 million (1.4%)
Total: $42.8 million

Tuition Fees

Undergraduate:
Full Time, Basic Fee - $4,029
Part Time - per course, Basic Fee - $806

Graduate Domestic Students:
Full Time - $5,304
Part Time - $2,652

Oshawa Campus
Fees paid on a per course basis - $806

Student/Teacher Ratio
- approximately one faculty member to every 27.4 students

International Students
- approximately 380 international students in 2001-2002 (2.4%, says Maclean's)

Undergraduate International Students Tuition Fees:
Full Time, Basic Fee - $4,029
  Differential Fee - $6,696
  Total Fee - $10,725
Part Time - per course, Basic Fee - $806
  Differential Fee - $1,339
  Total Fee - $2,145

Graduate International Students Tuition Fees:
Full Time, Basic Fee - $5,304
  Differential Fee - $6,202
  Total Fee - $11,506
Part Time - per course, Basic Fee - $2,652
  Differential Fee - $3,101
  Total Fee - $5,753

Women in Faculty

In 2000-2001 there were 182 full time faculty (>12 month appointments) of which 128 were males and 54 females.

Foodbanks on Campus
- one

Grants, Scholarships, Student Aid Programs

2000-2001
Scholarships - $576,400
Bursaries - $1,782,413
OSAP - $13,308,790
Work Study - $224,000 (government) plus additional 25% from Trent
Ontario Special Bursaries - $71,256
Special Needs Bursaries - $69,325

Child Care/Part Time Bursaries - $7,000

Aiming for the Top Scholarship - $99,000 (2000-2001)
$207,330 (2001-2002)

Millennium Scholarship - $10,000 (2000-2001)

"Success Stories"

Trent just recently decided to not build a privately owned or operated residence as part of their Build 2000 project - a project to renew and build on its suburban Symons Campus.

Students and faculty at Trent lobbied for months in opposition to the development of a privately owned or operated residence, culminating in the launch of the student union's GO PUBLIC, STAY PUBLIC campaign, in the concern that a private residential development could compromise the integrity of Trent's college system. This effort was successful, and after some consultation the university decided not pursue this option. This was a huge success for Trent in averting one particularly concerning mode of privatization.

Sessionals

Two unions cover faculty who teach less than full time. If you teach more than 1.5 courses you are under TUFA (Trent University Faculty Association). If you teach less than 1.5 courses you are in CUPE.❖

University finance in Canada: Into the 21st century
By Ron Melchers

In 1999-2000, Canada's universities continued their rapid climb out of the deep financial distress of the 1992-1997 period. However, as in recent years, this recovery has been felt in only a few areas of university expenditure: capital spending; sponsored research and endowments the most important among them.

In other areas, most especially revenues and expenditures related to teaching, resources have remained flat or have continued to decline. Increased student fees provided the only source of compensation for continued austerity in public support of teaching activities of universities. With enrolment all the while continuing to recover from decline earlier in the 1990s, students are now paying more than ever before for less and less per-student spending on their instruction and support.

Total revenues of Canada's 98 universities and university colleges reached $14.5 billion in 1999-2000, an increase of 18% over revenues of $12.2 billion in 1998-99. This is the largest single year-over-year increase ever reported. Not all of this increase, however, is new revenue. Changes in financial reporting rules introduced in 2000 permitted all universities to report sponsored research income and spending of non-consolidated entities, such as affiliated hospitals for example. Previously, reporting was not consistent across universities, with some reporting such expenditures and others not.

This change was in response to the increased use of standardized financial data in allocating federal research funding. It allowed for nearly $500 million of previously unreported sponsored research activity—more than half from private sources—to be added to university financial data. Nonetheless, even a resulting net increase of 15% in university income is still the most rapid annual increase in total university funding recorded since university financial data was first uniformly collected by Statistics Canada in 1972.

Capital stocks

The largest year-over-year increase was in government funding for capital additions by universities. New capital grants accounted for a quarter of all new revenues of universities. In 1998-1999, capital revenues of universities had reached a 20-year low as buildings constructed during the boom of the late 1960s and early '70s had deteriorated to the point of replacement for want of adequate maintenance and repair.

Total income for capital stock additions more than doubled in 1999-2000, led by more than $500 million in new public spending. The vast bulk of this new revenue came to Ontario universities through the first year of funding from the Ontario government's "SuperBuild" program. Atlantic, Alberta and Québec universities also experienced increases in capital funding, whereas capital funding for universities declined in British Columbia.

Sponsored research

The second most rapidly growing area of university revenues and expenditures is sponsored research, which grew to $2.6 billion in 1999-2000, up 21% from the previous year. Sponsored research activities now account for 18% of total university income and for 20% of new revenues in 1999-2000. Government funding, making up four-fifths of new money, led growth of sponsored research. Federal funding for research as a share of new revenues grew at a rate twice that of provincial funding. Although provincial funding for sponsored university research increased in all provinces, it did so most in Ontario (47%). Private sources contributed the remaining fifth of growth in sponsored research.

As in all other areas of university expenditure, growth is concentrated in infrastructure and operational costs, while human resource-related expenditures have failed to follow suit. Only 14% of new sponsored research spending in 1999-2000 is on wages, salaries and benefits, 8.6% in the case of Ontario universities.

Of course, much of the academic labour for sponsored research is paid out of general operating funds from provincial operating grants and student fees, rather than out of research grants or contracts. Equipment, operational supplies and expenses, and other infrastructure costs make up the largest and most rapidly increasing share of sponsored research spending.

Québec universities have been the largest beneficiaries of the growth in sponsored research. Although Québec universities take in 23% of all revenues to Canadian universities, they took in 29% of sponsored research revenues and 34% of new sponsored research revenues. Whereas sponsored research accounted for 20% of new revenues of all Canadian universities in 1999-2000, it accounted for 38% of new revenues of Québec universities.

Atlantic region universities, although taking in only 5% of Canadian university sponsored research revenues, experienced 9% of their net new revenues in sponsored research.

These changes are in part explained by the stagnation or decline in operating revenues, the largest source of university revenue. Research is a still growing activity in otherwise shrinking institutions.

University endowments

University endowments funds reached combined total assets of over $5 billion in 1999-2000, an increase of

19% over 1998-99, coming in equal portions from investment income and new donations.

General operations, instruction and non-sponsored research

General operating revenues of universities, which account for 57% of all revenues, grew by 7%, mainly as a consequence of nearly $200 million in increased tuition revenue. Nationally, tuition now provides 27% of total university operating revenues, while government operating grants provide 60%. General operations accounted for 52% of net new spending by universities.

Most new spending was for administrative supplies and equipment and administrative staff. Among sources of revenue, government operating grants saw virtually no growth, continuing a trend established since deep 1996-1997 cuts to operating grants. Only the three Prairie provinces bucked the national trend by increasing public support of university operations, by 8% in Alberta. Public support of university general operations, including teaching, declined 2% in both Québec and British Columbia.

Declining academic payrolls

Declines in public support for instruction and non-sponsored research were matched by declines in the academic payrolls of universities, for both full- and part-time academic rank faculty. This decline was -5% across all universities but –8% for research-inten-

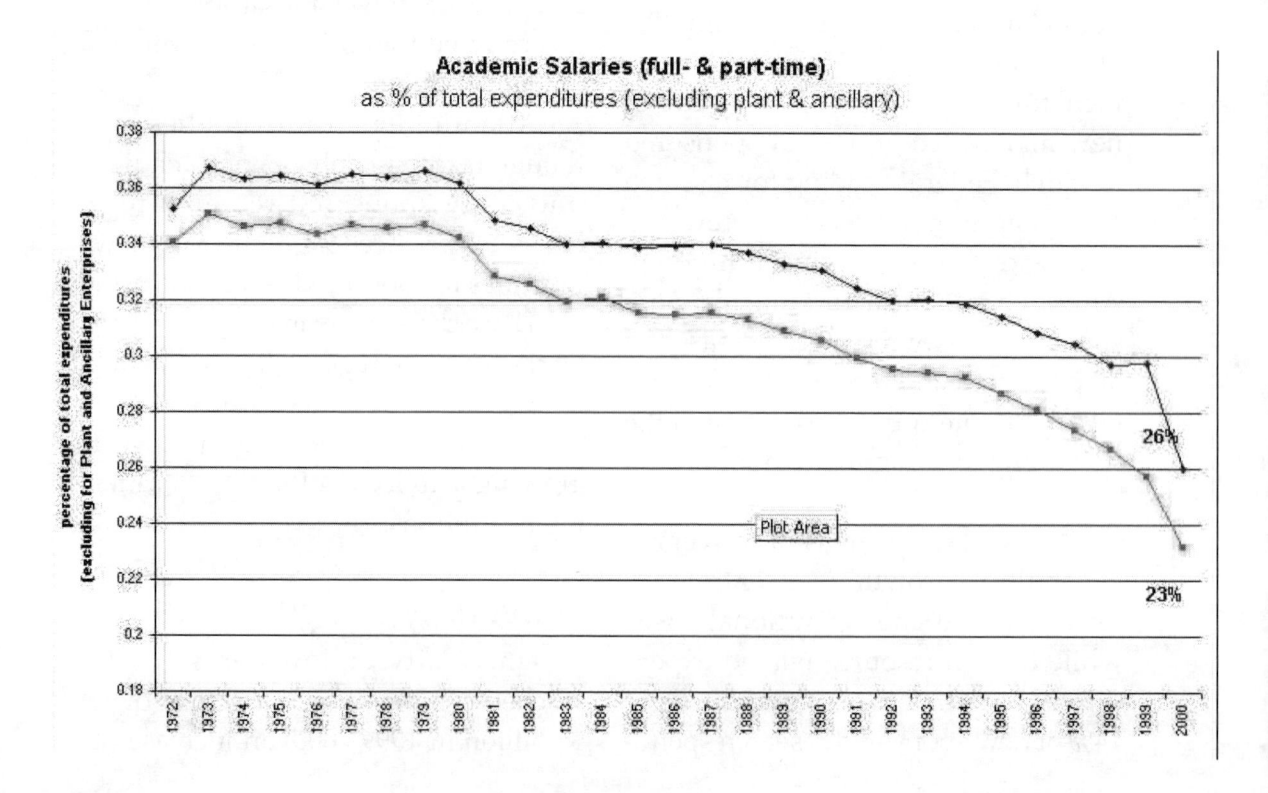

Academic Salaries (full- & part-time)
as % of total expenditures (excluding plant & ancillary)

sive universities and reaching –13% in Alberta.

This decline in academic rank payrolls is the consequence of two factors. The first, which has gone on largely unnoticed since the late 1970s, is the long-term decline of academic pay scales. The second, which has been much commented upon, is the beginning of a retirement boom in which a large cohort of highly-paid senior professors are either replaced by low-paid junior faculty or not replaced at all.

The issue of declining salary scales has gone largely unnoticed by both faculty themselves and their employers. This is because it has been directly experienced only by two groups of faculty: those coming into the profession at starting salaries that have lagged further and further behind those of most comparable professions; and those few faculty who have been at the ceiling of their pay scales for many years, who will have noticed that their earnings have been considerably eroded by inflation. All other faculty will have had the impression that pay is increasing as they have climbed up the pay scale, much as someone climbing stairs on the Titanic had the impression of keeping ahead of the waterline.

Unlike the Titanic, universities often have no one at their helm with either the interest or the ability to keep track of underlying features, other than on a sporadic basis. Employers have only noticed that their payroll costs had soared over the past decades as faculty aged up the pay scale. They have now only recently become aware of an impending retirement dividend.

In other work, this author has demonstrated that academic pay scales, as

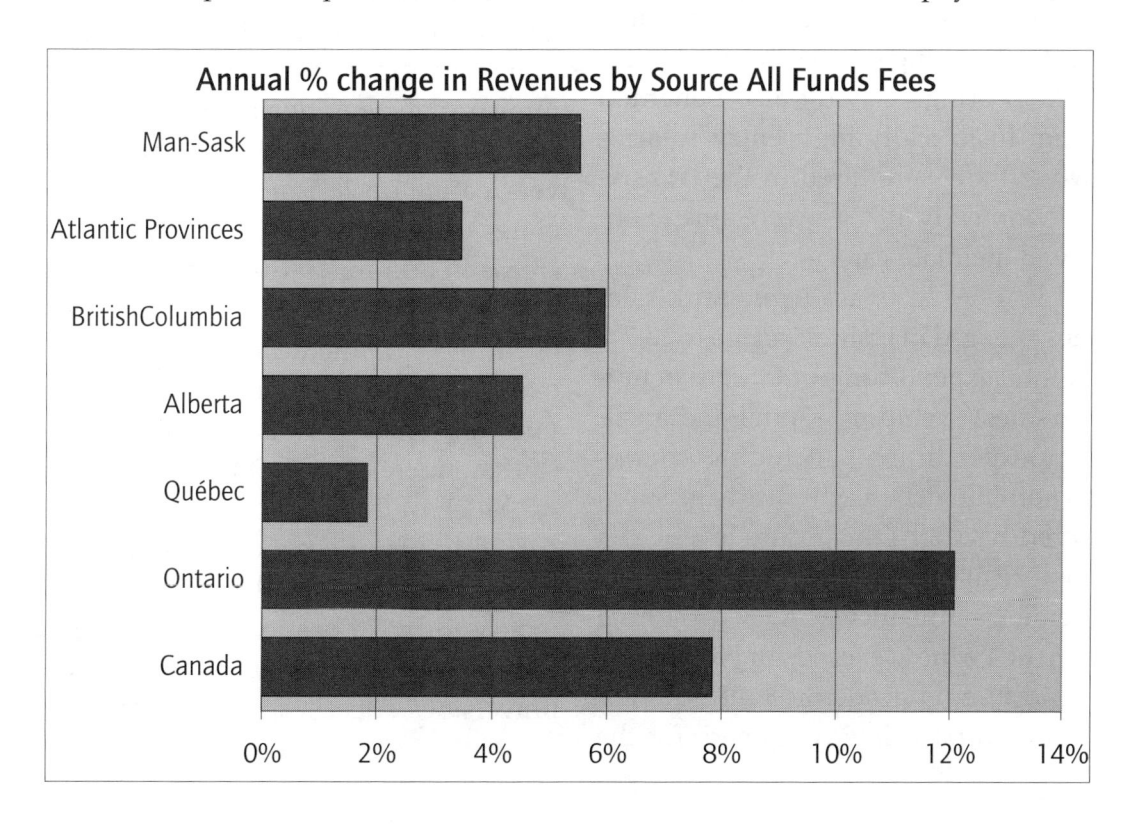

Annual % change in Revenues by Source All Funds Fees

Man-Sask	~5.5%
Atlantic Provinces	~3.5%
British Columbia	~6%
Alberta	~4.5%
Québec	~2%
Ontario	~12%
Canada	~8%

distinct from individual or aggregate salaries, have fallen nearly 20% in real dollar terms since peaking in 1977. David Balzarini, working with individual-level data, puts the peak at 1981, yet notwithstanding more movement over the years since, arrives at an even steeper long-term decline. This will mean that faculty payrolls will continue to fall rapidly over the next 10 years as a massive cohort of retiring faculty leave their experience increments behind, accelerated by the fact that faculty replacing them come into a considerably eroded career earnings structure.

Should increased competition for new faculty drive up hiring salaries, inter-generational inequities in career earnings will be exacerbated. This will be more so yet if faculty hired over the course of the past years of declining pay scales are asked to forgo the same higher finishing salaries that professors now retiring—having also benefited from historically high entry salaries when they were hired in the late sixties and early 1970s—were able to enjoy in their late careers.

In 1999-2000, academic rank salaries engaged in instruction fell to 23.2% of total expenditures of Canadian universities (excluding capital and ancillary expenditures). Including salaries in non-instruction activities (e.g., sponsored research) this figure is still at a historical low of 26%. The non-academic payroll, increasing at an annual rate of 4%, now exceeds university expenditure on academic rank salaries, full- and part-time combined, for the first time since financial information has been recorded for universities. This increase in non-academic salaries seems to have been largely confined to administrative operations: an annual increase of 30% in 1999-2000. Non-academic salaries in teaching operations fell –9% in 1999-2000.

Declining library resources

The stagnation of public support for university operations relating to teaching has also been felt in library acquisitions budgets. These have fallen by -2% nationally; by -7% for primarily undergraduate teaching universities; and by as high as -12% in Québec.

Increasing administration expenditures

The largest function increase in the general operating fund of Canadian universities is that of spending for administrative operations. This latter increased in 1999-2000 by 38% year-over-year, eating up 26% of all new net revenues of universities. Most of the increase in administrative expenditures within the general operating fund has been for equipment (increase of 65% over previous year) operational supplies (46% increase) and administrative staff (an increase of 30%).

Much of this phenomenon has occurred in Ontario, where administrative cost within general operations has increased by 70%, and furthermore is most noticed in the research-intensive universities. Alberta universities follow with a 56% increase in administrative costs.

From anecdotal evidence, we know that universities have increased considerably their activities in such areas as marketing and promotion, media relations, communications, student and faculty recruitment, and fund-raising. It remains to be seen whether this activity will benefit universities, or if it is only increasing competition in a zero-sum game.

Conclusion

Most of the historical trends noted in *Missing Pieces II* continued unabated in 1999-2000, with a two exceptions, that of the dramatic restoration of capital funding to universities, and the new emerging trend to significantly increase spending on administrative functions and staffing. Otherwise, the trends observed previously have all continued: higher tuition fees; declining or stagnant public contributions to the teaching activities of universities; a shifting of university resources to sponsored research led by increased federal spending; and the accompanying decline of university resources oriented towards education. Universities are going through a period of very rapid change. Whether or not this change serves Canadian society is an issue not receiving sufficient attention or debate.❖

What is a high quality education?
By Michael Temelini

I want to consider the meaning of the words 'quality' and 'high quality' when referring to education in Canada.[1] To help me through this difficult terrain, the celebrated political philosopher Charles Taylor offers a promising road map. Taylor writes that we may speak of 'institutions that serve' vs 'institutions that identify.' The former refers to structures that have a merely instrumental relation to our lives, even if the service they supply is very important (for example, a service station or a supermarket). The latter refers to the primary environments in which we define important values and hence our identity (for example, the family).[2]

'Institutions that identify' help us define what matters to us, where we elaborate our morality, where we discover and form our beliefs and principles as human agents. The contrast between these two types of institutions may help answer the question about what quality entails. First, I want to consider post-secondary educational institutions (our universities, colleges and CEGEPs[3]) as service stations, and suggest some limitations to this interpretation. Then I will explain why post-secondary institutions should be seen as institutions that identify. My intention is to clarify why the instrumental meaning of quality is neither synonymous nor identical with the substantive meaning.

❖ ❖ ❖

With reference to Canada's various institutions of post-secondary education, there are two ways in which the term 'quality' is typically used. One definition reduces education to a product or service. Again following Taylor, let's call this the "instrumental" definition since it assumes that the fundamental purpose of an educational institution is to efficiently deliver such products and services. Following this instrumental definition, an education of 'quality' depends on three related variables: the 'factors of production' (to borrow a term from economics); efficiency of delivery; and price. Let's consider each of these variables.

The educational factors of production may include a host of items: the academic and non-academic staff, as well as researchers and students that a post-secondary institution attracts. The number of students enrolled in each class is also important: whether there are limits on class sizes and limits on the ratio between students and professors. Other important factors are working conditions and wage levels for faculty, support staff, and teaching assistants. Factors also include the availability of capital and investment for libraries, for new technology, for research and sports facilities. These are important factors in defining the 'quality' of education as a service.

If the university or college is a service institution, then a quality education must also be related to efficiency. Efficiency has to do with how successfully the educational service is delivered to the 'customer' following the best cost-output ratio.[4] Hence the current vogue for on-line learning. According to the instrumental definition of education, quality is measured in terms of the institution's ability to offer the service in a way that generates profit or in which costs are adequately recovered, either by private funding (user fees, corporate investment, private donations) or grants from public sources.

Furthermore, what is often connected with this instrumental view is the belief, based on an interpretation of microeconomic theory, that the price system can be used as a tool to ensure or uphold quality. If educational institutions (the producers) are to deliver a high-quality product, so the argument goes, they must limit the quantity supplied to consumers and drive up the price. With higher prices the institution will have more capital to invest in or to upgrade its factors of production. In other words, quality is connected with restricted access to the product and increased price. The obvious flaw here is that in microeconomics the reason to limit supply is to maximize profit, not quality. Still, it is not uncommon to hear a justification for high user fees on the grounds that it will improve quality. Quality is linked to quantity, supplied or demanded.

The logic of this instrumental understanding of 'quality' is simple and compelling, particularly in an age when the operating principles of the market have held us captive. In fact, the debate about 'quality' can take place completely within the parameters of this instrumental definition of education. If we hold fast the fundamental principles of the instrumental view, then disagreements about quality education can only revolve around one or another factor of production, or around efficiency or around price.

For example, the Canadian student movement has traditionally championed the view that a high-quality education must be accessible, which is to say free of user fees and other non-financial barriers. It must also exhibit other important features: small student-teacher ratios; a large labour-intensive, well-trained work force, including tenured professors, teaching assistants, graduate researchers, and non-academic support staff; fair labour practices for all academic and non-academic staff, including a reasonable work schedule, a living wage, decent benefits, and the right to collective bargaining; and well-funded, easily accessible libraries and laboratories equipped with the latest technology and safety standards.

However compelling, the instrumental definition of education relegates outside of the picture other important aspects of education. For example, another way to understand the role of our institutions of post-secondary education has to do, not with the means, but with the purposes or aims of education. Let's call this the "substantive" definition, since what it presupposes is the view that educational institutions are not supermarkets, but environments that help us define what matters to us, to our sense of 'self.' Educational institutions are places where we articulate and debate our moral frameworks, where we discover and form our beliefs as citizens.

The idea here, in contrast to the instrumental view, is that our colleges, CEGEPs and universities embody and constitute our moral standards, ideals, visions of life, our shared and divergent social and political identities.

The distinction between instrumental and substantive definitions of quality education is more than merely academic. On the contrary, it is impossible to understand the movements for educational equity, democracy and justice if we cannot see this distinction. It helps explain the demands for democracy on governing boards and the demands for multicultural curricula. Our post-secondary institutions are supposed to be environments where students and educational workers deliberate on and learn about things that matter to them as members of a cultural community and a polity. This explains why some of the most significant demands for social change are often born on university and college campuses. It helps explain why the movements against corporate globalization have their most dedicated supporters on these campuses: because the educational institution is precisely the place where the moral outrage of our youth should be articulated.

When administrators and governors reject demands for diverse and multicultural curricula, deny greater democratic control and participation, invite corporate influence and control, and market their institutions as service centres, they are endorsing a way of life that is called into question by many students, professors, and support staff. When administrators condemn students for their activism because it hinders the delivery of the educational product or service, what is being challenged from the students' point of view is not just their equal role in the institution, but the recognition of their very identity. To paraphrase Taylor, it is hard for student activists to feel that they are really being given an equal role since what they stand for, their identity, is either invisible or being actively rejected.

Following this substantive definition of education, 'quality' can be defined in terms of the *kind* of education one is receiving. This definition refers to the quality of life that an educational institution embodies and promotes. It is also based on whether students, staff and faculty are able to participate fully in the university, not just as a mechanism that delivers a service, but as a shared community that upholds principles and values. In other words, this meaning of 'quality' takes into account whether the university or college is open to a variety of perspectives and curricula, and whether there is a place for common deliberation and public participation in decision-making.

I have been arguing that our colleges and universities cannot be seen or understood merely as instruments in the delivery of a service. If my argument is sound, if we accept the distinction between the instrumental and substantive definition of education, then a few things follow.

First, we have to reconsider the difference between 'quality' and 'high quality.' The difference cannot be based solely on factors of production. Furthermore, the definition of 'high quality' cannot be based either on the efficiency with which the educational institution delivers its service, or its price. Instead, a 'high-quality' education exists if—and only if—the educational institution promotes important substantive values. High quality is not something quantitative. It is not *more* quality. A high-quality education is defined in terms of the promotion of diverse curricula, equal participation, dialogue, understanding, knowledge, wisdom, tolerance, and achievement. To ensure a high-quality education, a university or college must be a space where students, professors, and support staff can debate and deliberate about what is good or right or honourable or just. To ensure a high-quality education, a university or college must defend and uphold the democratic values that the students, support staff and professors themselves are demanding.

The other conclusion that must follow from this argument is that we cannot have "high quality" without accessibility. An education of high quality can only be ensured by means of an open dialogue of various and dissenting voices. An education of high quality is one in which students are confronted by a broad diversity of values, cultures, and conceptual frameworks. Therefore, we cannot ensure a high-quality education by limiting access to education only to those who can afford it. On the contrary, high quality is best ensured by open and unfettered access.

Post-secondary institutions cannot be understood merely as instruments in the delivery of a service. They can be a mixture, in some ways closer to a service, while in others closer to structures of identity. But they cannot be reduced to service stations or supermarkets. Even if they deliver a service in the most efficient means possible, or deliver it at a very high price, we are still not justified in describing such a system of education as one of 'high quality.'

The Canadian post-secondary system must be accessible, and it must defend and promote the values of a peaceful, democratic and multicultural society. It must promulgate a curriculum that promotes the recognition and respect for human dignity and diverse forms of life. It need not promote relativism, nor the notion that all forms of life are incommensurable. But it would be sheer blindness not to recognize the fact that the struggle for 'high-quality' education is invariably associated not only or exclusively with service, efficiency and price, but also with substantive principles. ❖

Endnotes

1. I would like to thank Kevin Atkinson for his helpful comments on a draft of this essay.
2. Charles Taylor, "Institutions in National Life" in Charles Taylor, *Reconciling the Solitudes: Essays on Canadian Federalism and Nationalism* Edited by Guy Laforest. Montreal and Kingston: McGill-Queen's University Press, 1994. Taylor has devoted significanmt scholarly attention to the primacy of 'instrumental rationality' and how it displaces other forms of rational discourse. For example, see Taylor *The Malaise of Modernity* (Toronto: Anansi, 1991).
3. In Quebec after completing six years of elementary school and five years of secondary school, students are required to enroll in a unique post-secondary institution known as the Collège d'enseignement générale et professionnel or CEGEP (college of general and vocational education). The Cegeps were established in 1967 in Quebec to respond to the need for post secondary institutions that could train people for an advanced industrial society and prepare students wishing to pursue studies at University. The Cegeps were an important creation in the democratization and modernization of education in Quebec. The Cegeps offer two types of programmes: a two year pre-university diploma and three year technical career diploma, which prepares students to enter the job market. Regardless of their program, students take general education courses, some of which are common to all.
4. Taylor, *Malaise of Modernity*, 5.

Dumbing down distance education:
The corporate agenda and the end of quality
By Jennifer Sumner

While distance education has had a long association with corporations, it has rapidly moved with the development of information and communication technology to the very centre of the "education delivery" business to which global corporations are attracted. Distance education, once the poor cousin of higher education, has the potential to become a hugely profitable corporate commodity in a trend whose implications are seismic for both universities and world culture. The financial, trade and education departments of national and regional governments actively promote this corporatization of education, while denying they are doing so.

When describing the "shabby record" of distance education, David Noble[1] reminds us that correspondence instruction was a commercial enterprise before academia adopted it. By 1926, over 300 firms with well-developed sales forces flogged correspondence courses which 90% of the students failed to complete. Colleges and universities also staked their claims early in the 20th century. In the United States alone, 48 institutions were offering doctorates by correspondence, some of such dubious nature that correspondence study gained a tainted reputation that took decades to erase.[2]

At the beginning of the 21St century, distance education's intimate relationship with technology (course binders, audio tapes or videos) has catapulted it to prominence with the advent of home computers, e-mail and the Internet. These information and computer technologies have made possible the mass production of what is called "online learning." Since public budgets for education spending worldwide are estimated at US$2.2 trillion,[3] corporate interest in education is correspondingly avid. But as long as education remains a public good, it is inaccessible to private profiteering. Converting it to a private asset is thus the core of the corporate agenda for education.

Corporate globalization

Globalization is an ambiguous term that disguises the efforts of transnational corporations to commodify and profit from more and more aspects of our lives—from knowledge and leisure to death itself. Certain vital aspects of our lives are publicly funded, such as health care, education and old-age security, and this public funding prevents transnational corporations from cashing in on them. The corporate solution to this public protection is to demolish it through underfunding or outright abolition, paving the way for private takeover. This demolition is effected through policies that seek to lower corporate taxes and accommodate international flows of speculative capital, reduce public expenditures, and privatize public services, and deregulate business and secure monopoly private property rights under law.[4]

The World Trade Organization (WTO) is one of a number of supranational institutions that promote these policies, and its newest vehicle of policy enforcement is the General Agreement on Trade in Services (GATS). Under the GATS, education is considered a service, and as such is subject to two basic criteria. The first criterion puts the onus on governments to prove that public funding of this service is necessary, not on the WTO to prove that it is *not* necessary. The second criterion requires that all decisions made about services like education be "least trade restrictive," regardless of any other considerations.[5] With public funding judged a barrier to trade, public goods like education stand to be opened to corporate takeover over the next few years of GATS negotiations. How will this corporatization affect the quality of distance education?

The problem of quality

Online learning, whether publicly or privately owned, is the new frontier in distance education. And while using the Internet to transfer information is easy enough, little is known about the quality of the online education experience.[6] With the threat of corporatization, this unknown becomes amplified by the commodification process. The head of the Higher Education Funding Council for England, Sir Brian Fender, when looking for private-sector investors for a $300 million venture in "webucation," strove to assure the public that "quality, not price, is the crucial factor in webucation."[7] However, Canadian Professor Clare Polster warns that, "if you start seeing your course as a product, then you may become more concerned about its saleability than its quality."[8]

This warning takes on greater significance as distance educators align themselves with transnational corporations, which are bound by their fiduciary responsibility to increase shareholder value with every quarterly report. The drive to continuously increase profits while continuously decreasing costs will result in a learning experience that is compromised and stunted, subject to public-relations pressure tactics and consumer whims. The mismatch between the needs of education and the demands of the global market economy highlights the problem of quality when it comes to corporate distance education.

McMurtry[9] uses four categories to outline the contradictions between the guiding principles of education and of the capitalist market: goals, motivations, methods, and standards of excellence. These contradictions provide a fertile space for exploring the problem of quality in corporate distance education.

1. Goals

The overriding goal of corporate agents in the marketplace is to maximize private money-profits.

The overriding goal of educational agents in schools, colleges and universities is to advance and disseminate shared knowledge.

❖ ❖ ❖

The goal of maximizing private profit requires that knowledge not be shared, but privatized, packaged, and sold for a profit. The only knowledge that is advanced and disseminated is priced and packaged knowledge. The very saleability of distance education courses provides a temptation to commoditize all profitable knowledge and sell it to those who can afford it. While confusing quality with profitability, this commodification process deeply affects the kind of knowledge that is promoted, validated and accepted. It selects strictly for knowledge that can be computerized and sold. Other sorts of knowledge, such as knowledge constructed through social learning or knowledge hard-won through intellectual exploration or social struggle, are dismissed, invalidated, and rejected precisely because they can't be packaged and sold.

2. Motivations

The determining motivation of the market is to satisfy any want at all of anyone who has the money to purchase what is wanted.

The determining motivation of education is to satisfy the desire for knowledge of anyone who seeks it, whether they have the money to pay for it or not.

❖ ❖ ❖

The motivation to sell credentials through distance education courses to those who want to advance in the so-called "knowledge economy" will override questions of what constitutes quality in education. Quality becomes confused with professionalization, as job training takes precedence over other forms of education. In addition, satisfying the wants of those who can pay for this kind of education opens the door to distance education becoming a kind of entertainment in which quality is confused with the gratification of desires.

3. Methods

The method of the market is to buy or to sell ready-made products at whatever price one can get.

The method of education is never to buy or to sell its good to anyone, but to require of all who would have it that they fulfill its requirements autonomously.

❖ ❖ ❖

The corporatization of distance education risks turning institutions of higher learning into digital diploma mills[10] that churn out accreditation for a price. The higher the price, the less the chance that institutions will require paying students to fulfill educational standards.[11] No paying "consumers" anywhere else in the market are required to perform to spend. As ability to pay substitutes for ability to learn, quality is confused with quantity—number of students graduated and amount of money made.

4. Standards of excellence

The measures of excellence in the market are: a) how one-sidedly its own product-line is made to sell; and b) how problem-free the product is and remains for its buyer.

The measures of excellence in education are: a) how inclusively it takes into account others' interests and avoids one-sided biases; and) how deep and broad the problems it poses are to one who has it.

❖ ❖ ❖

Distance education that caters to narrow, corporate concerns excludes the possibility of critical voices and alternative visions. Confusing quality with problem-free promotion of corporate interests, such corporatized distance education ignores the question of bias, and discourages critique. Education without a range of understandings to choose from or a critical orientation verges on indoctrination, eliminating the possibility of perspective transformation that grappling with deep and broad problems can lead to.

The move to quality control

There is no doubt that distance education has many advantages. People can learn on their own time, in their own home, at their own pace. Distance education can benefit people in remote areas, people with employment obligations, or people confined in one place. But it is strictly a supplement to, never a substitute for, the face-to-face engagement and open critical debate that permits the kind of deep and questioning learning that is the hallmark of all quality education.

In the midst of the current scramble for cash by university administrators, the prestigious Massachusetts Institute of Technology (MIT) has announced that it will make most of its teaching materials available for free on the Internet—taking a clear stand against the privatization of knowledge on which corporate distance education depends. This counter-corporate move testifies to a new awareness that "there is far more to learning than mere "content," that education is not a branch of the infotainment business, and that maybe there is a point in having real universities rather than virtual diploma mills."[12]

The corporate agenda for education clearly compromises the quality of distance education. Transnational corporations have no place in key aspects of life such as education, where academic, not economic, considerations must determine the quality of education.❖

Endnotes

[1] Noble, David. 2000. "Comeback of an Education Racket." *Le Monde Diplomatique*, April, p. 15.

2. Portman, David. 1978. *The Universities and the Public: A History of Higher Adult Education in the United States*. Chicago: Nelson-Hall, p. 33.
3. *CanadExport*, September 1999, p.16.
4. The Globalism Project. 2001. Parkland Institute, University of Alberta, Canada. Available at: www.ualberta.ca/~parkland/mcri.html.
5. Sanders, Richard. 2001. "GATS: The End of Democracy?" *Australian Financial Review*, June 15, p. 6 of Review Section.
6. Press, Eyal and Jennifer Washburn. 2001. "Digital Diplomas." *Mother Jones*, January/February, pp. 34-39, 82-83.
7. In Donald MacLeod. 2001. "Cashing in on Clever Business Plans." *Guardian Weekly*, January 11-17, p. 24.
8. In Tema Frank. 2001. "Online Courses: A Gold Rush or Fool's Gold?" *University Affairs*, February, p. 13.
9. McMurtry, John. 1998. *Unequal Freedoms: The Global Market as an Ethical System*. Toronto: Garamond.
10. Digital diploma mills is a concept used by education critic David Noble to highlight the dangers of the increasing corporatization of education (see David Noble. 1998. Digital Diploma Mills: The Automation of Higher Education." *CAUT Bulletin*, Spring, Fall).
11. Universities offering MBA programs are getting squeamish about whether their elite students should be tested or whether a CEO should be failed (see Erika Shaker. 1999. "Higher Education, Limited: Private Money, Private Agendas." *Education, Limited*, Vol. 1, No. 4. Ottawa: The Canadian Centre for Policy Alternatives, p. x).
12. Naughton, John. 2001. "Well Webucated?" *Guardian Weekly*, May 3-9, p. 24.

Post September 11 afterword
By David Noble

The following is the afterword to Digital Diploma Mills: The Automation of Higher Education, by David Noble (copyright 2002). This book was published in Canada by Between the Lines (http://www.btlbooks.com) and in the United States by Monthly Review Press (http://www.monthlyreview.org).

In the first article in this series (Chapter Two of this volume) I noted that online delivery of university courses rendered all course content and communication transparent to parties beyond the direct participants, in violation of the privileged relationship between teachers and students. I pointed out, for example, that web-based courses at UCLA, the first major university to mandate websites for all of its liberal arts courses, were routinely audited by the administration and that websites were typically created and updated by a cadre of administration-appointed technicians rather than by the instructors themselves; that UCLA's partner in online delivery, the Home Education Network (later Onlinelearning.net) regularly monitored their online offerings; that distance-education administrators at the University of Colorado were able to oversee their courses in progress as readily as if they were sitting at the back of the classroom; that, according to its designer, Marvin Goldberg, the popular WEB-CT courseware platform allowed for "lurking" by third parties as well as the automatic storage and retrieval of all online activities; and that the Virtual U courseware platform designed at Simon Fraser University automatically collected usage data, and conference transcript data (from chat rooms and other e-mail communications) for the use of systems developers.

In light of such transparency, I asked readers to consider "what third parties will have access to [course] communications?"

At the time I was concerned about surreptitious administrative and commercial monitoring of students and instructors, as an invasion of privacy and a mechanism for evaluation, intimidation, and the appropriation of intellectual property. But recent events have given new meaning and urgency to this question about online spying practices and capabilities. In the aftermath of September 11, governments have vastly enlarged their powers of surveillance, and surveillance of electronic communication in particular. Moreover, as we have seen, the U.S. military itself has now become the single largest consumer of university-based online instruction.

With or without university administration compliance, government agencies are able as never before to monitor, access, and subpoena university course content and communications for alleged security purposes. The past record of university administrators in protecting faculty against such government actions is less than encouraging, as Cold War experience suggests.[1] Indeed, even before the attacks on the World Trade Center, the content and syllabi of courses offered by professors of the State University of New York (SUNY) system had become subject to political review by the Board of Trustees. Recent disclosures indicate that the University of Toronto has been the site of administration-sanctioned spying on faculty by Canada's CIA, the CSIS. At my own university, documents have just surfaced showing that the current Vice-President (Academic) compiled lists of faculty participating in demonstrations during a legal strike.

Since September 11, such threats to academic freedom and free speech have multiplied dramatically. At California State University at Fresno a dean provided the Air Force with a list of foreign students without their knowledge or consent; at UCLA a librarian who had sent a critical e-mail response to a colleague's political message was summarily suspended; at the University of New Mexico, a professor who made an offhand remark to students in his class about the September 11 attacks has been vilified by state legislators and his own administration and charged with unprofessional conduct; at California State University in Chico, a faculty member was deluged with hate mail for posting questions about U.S. foreign policy; at the City University of New York, participants in a teach-in sponsored by the Professional Staff Congress, the faculty union, were assailed by state politicians, the press, and the chancellor and trustees of the CUNY system for allegedly anti-American statements. And in Canada, a professor at the University of British Columbia was vilified by federal and provincial politicians and the national and local press for critical remarks she made about U.S. foreign policy at a conference of women's service organizations, and charged by the national police, the RCMP, with committing a hate crime.

This is just the beginning. It appears that we are at the start of a wholesale state-sponsored assault on civil liberties, if "anti-terrorist" legislation enacted in the United States and Canada is any indication. The squeeze on academic freedom is just a small part of this process. But in this deepening crisis and its attendant security-conscious climate, the transparency of online instruction becomes not merely a matter of academic but of far larger political concern. Certainly administrators and political authorities will be in a position to monitor any and all such activities as never before, remotely and discreetly, without permission or acknowledgment, and they will have ready access to extensive electronic records of course content and communications.

Of course, we all believe we have nothing to hide, that what we or our students say online to one another is not only beyond reproach or suspicion, but without any real significance. Why would anyone care about what goes on in my courses? But if the past is any guide, and it might well be, we should heed the hard-won lesson that in the end, in times such as these, guilt and suspicion are in the eye of the beholder.❖

Endnotes

[1] See, for example, Ellen Schrecker's account of academia's response to the McCarthy period, in her *No Ivory Tower*.

The university as a workplace in the global context
By Teresa Healy

The privatization of universities has become a key component of economic restructuring carried out by provincial and federal governments and promoted by globalized business interests. In Canada, university workers have faced severe pressures on wages and working conditions and acquired collective rights. At the same time, university workers and their community allies have organized to fight back against privatization.

Introduction

As governments have restructured the economy according to post-Fordist ideals promoted by global capital, the state itself has been the focus of restructuring as well. From the perspective of the labour movement, some of the key dynamics of state restructuring in Canada may be understood by analyzing changes in the production of public services. The new management obsession with increasing the amount of value-added per hour worked has meant that the reduced workforce faces a dramatically increased workload.

The Canadian Union of Public Employees' research on workload has shown how this has resulted, not just in the extension and intensification of the working day, but in workers bearing the brunt through injuries, increases in stress-related illnesses, and startling rates of unpaid overtime worked by union members.[1]

In the public sector, however, the implications of this restructuring of work is not simply a matter for workers. It is a matter of grave significance for the community we serve. After years of underfunding in the post-secondary education sector, for example, the public is growing anxious. A recent IPSOS-Reid poll commissioned by CUPE and other members of the Ontario-based Post-secondary Education Coalition shows that 70% of Ontario parents are concerned (43% very concerned) that their kids may not be able to attend university or college, even if they are qualified and choose to do so. For the vast majority (79%) of parents, cost is the overriding factor as to why they are concerned. By all accounts, over the next decade, there will be a dramatic increase in the number of potential students in postsecondary education institutions in Ontario. Two-thirds (64%) of Ontario parents would rather the government increase provincial government funding for universities and colleges, even though this may result in a cancellation of planned tax cuts or reduced government spending in other areas. Only 16% chose the establishment of private universities and colleges throughout the province, and smaller proportions chose raising student entrance requirements to universities and colleges to restrict the number of students admitted (12%) and increasing student tuition fees to universities and colleges (6%).

The release of the findings of this poll came on the heels of an Ipsos-Reid poll which showed that education ranks as the second most important issue on the public agenda, only 1% behind health care[2].

For public sector workers, work intensification and the underfunding of social programs are very clearly linked. Both are contributing to a process of privatization intended to bring public services directly under the control of a highly globalized private sector. But the process of privatization is not unidirectional. Public sector workers and their community allies have been part of the history of state restructuring, given their conscious acts of resistance, collective bargaining strategies and mobilization.

What becomes evident from an analysis of privatization in the university sector is the extent to which all levels of government are committed to using the instruments of the state to restructure educational services. At the same time, this restructuring of post-secondary education further restructures the state itself and creates a highly polarized civil society, both in terms of ideological conflict and the distribution of economic resources.

To show how the restructuring of post-secondary education is bound up with the restructuring of the state, we shall examine the university as a site of production. For employers, it holds the potential to be a location for the production of ideology as well as significant surplus. For university workers, it holds potential as a site for the construction of counter-hegemony arising from the defence of collective agreements and coalition building that contest the terms of state restructuring.

The four major issues facing university workers are 1) efforts by elected national leaders to change the character of the state by forging international agreements and use every instrument at its disposal to bring the university sector under the discipline of the market; 2) efforts by provincial governments to bring market relations into all areas of the university (underfunding; public-private partnerships; private research funding; deregulation of tuition; competitive bidding; franchising, introduction of private for-profit universities); 3) efforts by employers to change the organization of work in the university (benchmarking; workload increases; casualization); and 4) efforts by university workers to resist and transform these conditions.

Federal government and international agreements

On April 18, 2001, the draft FTAA chapter on investment was leaked and circulated internationally. CUPE Research has completed an initial study of this chapter.[3] What we see confirms our previous analysis of trade and investment deals as elaborated in this year's chapter on trade and public services from our *Annual Report on Privatization*.[4] If approved, the implications of the FTAA for public services will be far-reaching.

Proponents of liberal trade and investment agreements argue that the state has plenty of room to act within the scope of both NAFTA and the draft FTAA. Government leaders suggest that public services are protected by ongoing negotiations of the General Agreement on Trade in Services (GATS) as well as the Free Trade Area of the Americas. To make their case, they refer to Article 1 of the NAFTA investment chapter. This article indicates that governments have the exclusive right to activities listed in Annexes, created by member governments. Governments also have the right "to refuse to permit the establishment of investment in such activities" (1101:2). The problem, however, is that Article 1 also says that a government is permitted to offer services, *providing it does so in a manner consistent with the Chapter*. Furthermore, given the political dynamics of the last 15 years or so, privatization is increasing in the public sector in most countries of the Americas. In Canada, there are few services left that are provided exclusively by the government.

The FTAA draft investment chapter includes all of the above and also suggests a new paragraph in Article 1. Notwithstanding a government's right to provide services, *if an investor of a Party provides similar services, the investments of that investor shall be protected by this Chapter*. Because there is no bracketed text accompanying this draft paragraph, we know there is no debate among the parties on this point.[5] As well, the FTAA Article 1 includes an uncontested paragraph compelling all levels of government to comply with the Chapter[6]. If we look carefully at Article 1, the case made by advocates of free trade and investment starts to look quite shaky.

The investor-state provisions of NAFTA for the first time allowed corporations to sue states if they wished to argue that their rights under the treaty were not fulfilled. This marked a clear shift in the terms of international law, which had considered states to be the legitimate parties to agreements, and therefore the only legitimate interlocutors of disputes arising. Not any more. Private investors can use the investor-state dispute resolution provisions of NAFTA to challenge the so-called "unfair competition" by the government in its support for the public sector, for example. It appears likely that the FTAA will contain the same provisions, and it also appears likely that we will see more cases like Metalclad vs the Mexican government,

UPS vs Canada, and Ethyl Corp vs Canada.

There can be no doubt that the FTAA draft investment chapter is meant to entrench and expand the rights of private investors. Only a few years ago, it was widely agreed that certain things should not be bought and sold. Today, governments of the world's most powerful countries have decided to bring public services under the discipline of the market. Increasingly, the public sector is constrained by the expansion of market relations and the process of commodification, bringing many more aspects of social provision directly under corporate control.

The federal government and the disciplining of PSE

The expansion of market relations does not, however, simply roll over us like an early morning fog. It is an expansionary process driven by the globalized interests of the owners of capital and facilitated by neoliberal governments in their restructuring of the state. In Canada, for example, the federal Liberals have cut over $3 billion in federal transfers for post-secondary education. Because of chronic underfunding, however, at least $3.6 billion is needed to repair university infrastructure and physical plant across the country.

The federal government has reduced education funding in its deficit, tax, and debt reduction frenzy. But this has been accompanied by an equally vigorous promotion of private funding and corporate investments in post-secondary education. The Canadian Federation of Students reports that tuition has increased 126% in the past decade. The average debt load for students has increased to $25,000 and is still increasing.

The Liberal government increased Canadian Health and Social Transfer cash payments in this mandate, but has not re-established program financing to the levels that existed prior to its severe cuts in transfers in the mid-1990s. Further, the Liberals maintained the transfer of tax-points to the provinces, making it virtually impossible to forge agreements on national standards on accessibility.[7] We cannot know how much of CHST money is directed to post-secondary education. The Canadian Association of University Teachers (CAUT) estimates that federal transfers to colleges and universities have been cut by more than 20% since 1991, while provincial transfers have declined 12% and university and college revenues from tuition fees have increased by 40%.[8] All of our scenarios indicate that the money allocated is insufficient, especially since absolute numbers do not factor in increased costs due to population growth and inflation.

Instead of working against tuition-fee hikes, the Liberal government established Millennium scholarships and a Registered Education Savings Plan that, apart from being an inadequate response to the magnitude of the problem, keeps the pressure on families to bear the costs of their children's education, benefits the financial sector, and privatizes what we think of as a social obligation.

After years of complaints from Canada's chartered banks, the federal Liberals took back responsibility for student loans, but then passed it over to two private firms to do so. Edulinx Canada and BDP have now been designated as the administrators of the Canada student loans program.[9] Alternatively, 16 other countries in the Organization for Economic Cooperation and Development (OECD) offer free tuition for colleges and universities.

One of the ways in which the federal government is supporting the privatization of Canadian universities is through the systematic underfunding of the Social Sciences and Humanities Research Council, together with the creation of a new research funding body, the Canadian Foundation for Innovation (CFI). The CFI was allocated $900 million in the 2000 budget, bringing federal investment in the Foundation to $1.9 billion until 2005.[10] The money was to be used to fund research infrastructure in Canadian universities, but is also serving as a tool for restructuring. University applicants must demonstrate that they have private partners and other public partners willing to put up 60% of project funding. In this way, corporate interests are able to decide who the research is for, and to what purpose it will be put.[11] In the words of the CFI, the "partnerships… have been crucial not only in mobilizing the matching funds, but also in helping researchers and institutions to develop higher quality, more innovative proposals."[12]

Here we must stop to point out why one can rarely hear any representative of the federal government refer to post-secondary education without using some form of the word "innovation" as well. "Innovation" is not a synonym for "creativity." This is because the federal government has accepted the language of the Expert Panel on the Commercialization of University Research. Innovation is defined as: "the process of bringing new goods and services to market, or the results of that process."

The Liberal government argues it means to combine "strategic new investments" in PSE along with tax-cuts. The assumption is that tax cuts to knowledge-intensive sectors will build a strong economy. The Liberals argue that a fiscally responsible government promoting a favourable tax regime for R&D will help ensure competitiveness in a global marketplace where other countries are investing in R&D and life-long education of their workforce. This part of the privatization agenda is meant to bring universities into line with corporate objectives.

Given this frenetic level of activity by the federal government in an area of provincial jurisdication, one might wonder when Section 92 of the Constitution was to be invoked. Interestingly, it was not a provincial premier who recently raised an objection. In a press conference held during the April 2001 Summit of the Americas, Prime Minister Chrétien was asked a question about the introduction of private universities to Canada. The questioner asked the Prime Minister whether the critics of DeVry or the University of Phoenix were right to be concerned about the opening up of education to the FTAA and market forces. The Prime Minister responded by saying that

> ...our system of universities in Canada is a well-known one and we intend to maintain the way it is. If you want to start a school yourself, and charge for it, I don't know, it's completely forbidden. But I don't know what you are referring to. It's not a major problem. Because if some Americans are coming to offer some programs here, I don't know of it.

He then listened to a supplementary question restating the link between services and international trade and investment deals, and said:

> But I'm telling you that you talking about the government of Alberta. You ask them the question. I am not the one that decides these things in Canada, it is not my responsibility.[13]

As the Prime Minister declined to talk about the impact of globalisation, trade and investment on the people of Canada, federalism was used as a defence against democracy.

Global capital: The case of Thomson Corporation

To set these changes at the international and national level into perspective, we need to consider the driving force behind them. To do this, we will take as an example the case of the Thomson Corporation. The year 2000 was a big one for Thomson Corporation. In February, the long-time publisher (first incorporated in Ontario in 1977) announced it would sell all of its interests in newspapers, except for the Globe and Mail. The company made the decision to leave print media in to the dust-bin of history, and turn its attention to the twenty-first century world in which it aims to be "the world's foremost, global e-information and solutions company".

The Corporation has spent approximately $ 5.7 billion U.S. in the past 5 years, to buy up new businesses. Its largest acquisition was West Publishing Company, a US publisher of legal and educational materials, and provider of electronic information services, for which it paid U.S. $3,425 billion in 1996. In March 2000, Thomson acquired Prometric, a company developing computer-based testing and assessment services.

This "Canadian" company now earns 93% of its income in the United States. With revenues of 5.5 billion, half of which were electronic-based (including $390 million in Internet-based revenues), Thomson is a big player in the education marketplace. Thomson Learning intends to profit from the $6 billion academic market, including secondary, post-secondary and graduate education. It also intends to make its mark in the $5.1 billion life-long learning market, and the $14 billion "outsourced US corporate training market", including distance education, information technology and language instruction. Global education spending is estimated at $1.5 trillion, is expected to double in the next five years and double again in the five years after that. E2C (education to consumer) and E2B (education to business) is big news.

Provincial governments: Administrative renewal or the corporate restructuring of work?

Since coming to power in 1995, the Conservative Government in Ontario has embarked upon a radical restructuring of the province's educational system. Latterly, post-secondary education has been one of the key targets in the Government's sights. Most dramatically, in the autumn of 2000, the Government introduced legislation permitting the establishment of for-profit private universities in Ontario. Bill 132 permits corporations to apply to open private for-profit PSE institutions. We expect private, for-profit universities to increase student fees dramatically and decrease accessibility. We also expect that this move will change the character of the post-secondary education system because of its potential to contribute to a "tiered" post-secondary educational system affecting both colleges and universities. Furthermore, once private institutions are part of the PSE system, it is likely that international trade and investment laws will open up a whole new area of conflict in which the Ontario government could be accused of "discriminating" against foreign corporations by virtue of its support for public post-secondary institutions.

The introduction of for-profit Universities has not been the only move towards privatization, however. Slowly but surely, public-private partnerships have been introduced into the Provinces colleges and universities. For example, under the Ontario government's "R&D Challenge Fund", public research money is allocated to universities only after they have identified a private partner. As well, R&D firms are given tax cuts in exchange for associating with a university. Perhaps more insidious is the Access to Opportunities Fund (ATOP). In 1998, the Ontario government began to promote private sector investments to create spaces for students in Colleges and Universities. The government gave $150 million for a three year program to create 17, 000 new spaces for students in computer science and engineering. In July 1999, the program was expanded to a target of 23, 000 students. The government committed $228 million while the private sector invested $136 million. The funds are considered part of total operating grants.

Early in 2000, we began to hear how Ontario would benefit from the "largest capital investment in Ontario's colleges and universities in more than 30 years". Public and private "SuperBuild" funds have been allocated to renew our decaying infrastructure on campus. SuperBuild Corporation forecasts $1 billion to be spent in PSE over five years, together with $800 million in private investment. Recently, the Ontario government released a report of SuperBuild's first year. In Ontario, public-private partnerships and capital infrastructure projects are now directed by the Cabinet Committee on Privatization and SuperBuild.

SuperBuild public-private partnership has committed to establish 73,000 new student spaces with a $1 billion investment by the government, and $0.8 billion investment by private sector (Paper E, p. 177). Given that the government is dramatically undercounting the number of new students expected to enter the system, it is likely that new spaces will fall short by 15,000. Post-secondary educational institutions are expected to find space by seeking out increased efficiencies. The government allocated an unexpected $140 million in 2000-01 for the renovation of existing post-secondary facilities (Paper E, p. 177), far less than what is needed to renovate and accommodate student demand.

The most recent Ontario Budget indicates that the push towards privatization is continuing at full-speed. Infrastructure continues to be a central target. The Ontario Financial Review Commission will report to the Minister of Finance on the government's capital assets in order to track historic costs, replacement value, asset condition and deferred maintenance needs (Paper E, p. 155, 157). Colleges and Universities are required to submit capital plan and investment reports. This is part of the government's strategy to see whether "it has the right mix of assets and whether its capital investment strategy will lead to the desired policy outcomes" (Budget Paper E, p. 158).

The Budget reports an expenditure of $100 million in funding for deferred maintenance at Ontario's post-secondary institutions during the year 2000-01 (Budget Paper B, p. 43). This was a one-time expenditure not foreseen in last year's Budget. But this is simply not enough money. The Canadian Association of University Business Officers reports it would cost $1.06 billion to pay for deferred maintenance at Ontario universities alone. That's over $4,200 per student and more than 10 times what the government delivered in 2000-01. There is no new money in the 2001-02 Budget for deferred maintenance.

The chronic problem of underfunding has not yet been resolved. The Budget indicates there will be an increase in post-secondary operating grants by an estimated $293 million by 2003-04 (Budget Paper B, p. 53). What does this mean? Let's look at enrolment increases closely. It is assumed there will have been a 16.3% increase in enrolment in Ontario's Universities between 1995-96 when this government came to power and 2003-04. During the same time, funding will have gone up by only 7.4%. If we were to count the effect of inflation on the value of the dollar, the increase would even be less. This is why the Ontario Confederation of University Faculty Associations (OCUFA) says the government is only funding the increase in enrolment at about 50 cents on the dollar. According to OCUFA's analysis, in 1995-96, operating grants to Universities were $1.814 billion. The government is projecting $1.948 billion for 2003-04. OCUFA reports we can expect a decline of 22.9% in real dollars per full-time equivalent student funding between the academic year 1995-96 when the Harris government took power, and 2003-04 when the spending estimates for post-secondary education end.

In Ontario's Universities, privatization is taking shape through the introduction of for-profit universities, public-private partnerships, tied operating and capital funding, as well as by the pressures introduced through underfunding, but that is not the end of the story. The process of privatization is also changing the way in which work is done at the University. On September 19, 2000 the Ontario Government formed the "Investing in Students Taskforce". It called for proposals to "increase administrative effectiveness and efficiencies" by examining "best practices in administrative operations and related expenditures in Ontario and other jurisdictions."

In the University environment, 'administrative operations' can include student financial aid administration; facilities planning, maintenance and utilisation; purchasing; human resources; information technology, including data collection and web-based services; retail operations and ancillary services; registration processes and practices; counselling services; finance and reporting. This list of activities affects all aspects of the University. It is not incidental. It is fundamental to University workers, because it is our work that is being restructured.

The Taskforce had a mandate to accept proposals fostering private-public partnerships, promote "fundamental change" in administration, establish ways to measure efficiency, save money, avoid costs and reduce red tape, including proposals proposing the disposition (selling) of assets. Through this taskforce, the government is looking for ways to privatize University services. Early in 2000, the employers' organization, Council of Ontario Universities, committed to conduct "annual evaluation of whether to keep or to contract-out ancillary operations". Through the winter, the COU took the lead on coordinating University submissions to the Taskforce.

The Ontario Government released the Taskforce Report on March 20, 2001. The Taskforce focuses its attention on the "needs of students', but in this instance, "students" is a synonym for "customers". Throughout the Report, the Taskforce recommends Universities adopt business practices in every aspect of University Administration. When we actually consider students as "students", the top problem causing debate is the high level of student fees. The Taskforce's response was to recommend credit counseling for students, rather than tuition freezes and rollbacks, or a grants program. In its most recent budget, brought down on May 9th, the Conservative government congratulated itself because it had "raised" $600 million to assist students over 10 years. Why is the government "raising" money for student assistance when it is giving away billions of dollars in tax cuts? The Budget documents reports that "Ontario's general rate of corporate income tax is being reduced from the highest among industrialized countries to a level below all U.S. states" (Paper C, p. 82). Furthermore, corporations will be permitted tax-based incentives for research and development that undermine Federal Government taxation policies (Paper C, p. 97).

Benchmarking is a process of standardization of the processes involved in the production of goods and services. International standards organizations continue to facilitate standardization in way we work, in order to increase productivity. Standardization is meant to increase the level of "value-added" in each phase of the production process. contributes to contracting out and privatization, as well as the intensification of the working day, and efforts to 'flexibilize' the labour force. It is likely that Committee to review benchmarking will not include representatives from labour. The report offers no recommendations that come from labour. Nor do they even recognise the University as a workplace.

Many problems arise for CUPE members who must work in these "leaned-out" University workplaces, among them the pressure for give-aways to employers, dangerous working conditions because of deferred maintenance, downward pressure on wages and working conditions because of the comparison with newly privatized facilities on campus, and increased workload and stress because of the chronic reduction of resources to do the work that needs to be done.

The Taskforce recommends E-Learning on a 24/7 basis. Will these tutorial and other services be delivered by contingent workers or unionized, decently paid workers with good working conditions? Where will they work? Will they ever see their co-workers? Will they be able to bargain collectively with their employer? Will they be home-workers? What will their conditions of work be? How many hours will they work? How will their wages be determined? The Taskforce further recommends different post-secondary institutions share services in order to achieve greater efficiencies. This sounds reasonable, but on what basis will this occur? Will rationalizing the use of resources mean contracting-out and further privatization?

Thompson's strategy fits well with the current thinking on the part of employers. The reason "competency-based," rather than "class-room hours" accreditation has become popular among employers is that these courses can be delivered on an individual basis, on-line and through distance education. Under these conditions, it becomes possible for the worker to continuously upgrade on his or her own time. It's the ultimate in flexibilized private education. Flexible, that is, for the employer.

Given the tremendous time pressures faced by working people, regular College and University class schedules and locations make it difficult for many people to enrol and complete post-secondary education. Distance and on-line training might offer some alternatives. But we have to remember that it is not the technology itself which will determine whether distance education is democratic. It depends upon how that technology is used and for what purposes. Under close examination, the bright presentation of "life-long learning" begins to look somewhat tarnished. Does "life-long learning" present working people with an opportunity or an added demand? Does distance education offer employers a way out of on-the job training or time off the job? How will women with children or aging parents have time to up-grade in the evenings and on weekends? Given the fact that women continue to be responsible for an unequal share of domestic responsibilities, are women workers going to be left out of 'life-long learning'? These are all questions that will need to be addressed as we face these changes.

We can see how private universities would welcome this form of education. If this service can be delivered outside of the classroom, then there is no need for buildings to be built, heated or maintained. There's no grass to cut, physical plant to be attended to, or floors to be cleaned. No snow to clear, walls to be painted or unions to be dealt with. You get the picture. Does the University community recognize, as it forays into distance education, IT and language certification, businesses consider them to be delivering 'outsourced corporate training'? Let's consider that phrase for a moment. Outsourcing refers to the process by which some aspects of the production process are contracted-out of the main production facility to an enterprise farther down the supplier chain. In other words, the supplier depends on the demands of those higher up in the production hierarchy. The phrase 'outsourced corporate training' is evocative. With great clarity, it captures the vision corporations have for the place of universities in society. Corporations may providing their own training, but it is increasingly likely that employees will be responsible for their own accreditation, when they can find it, from for-profit institutions or publicly supported colleges and Universities.

Across the country, untenured, part-time contract faculty are responsible for an ever - increasing%age of university teaching. Part-time faculty are the university's contingent workforce. Without a union they have little job security, few benefits and low wages. Yet their workloads increase as universities fail to replace retiring permanent faculty. Sessional instructors are no longer considered 'professors-in-training'. They are flexible, highly productive and dispensable workers. Casualization is not unusual in this sector. Statistics Canada reports that of all non-permanent job types, education and related services ranks first at 15.1%. About 1.8% of non-permanent workers are located in the retail trade sector. Health and welfare services rank third at 10.3% and accommodation and food services is next at 8.6 per cent.

Why do our employers want more flexibility and increased productivity? Governments have under-funded and restructured public services according to private sector values. They may want to prepare public services to be privatized or they may wish to avoid being accused of unfairly subsidizing services that corporations wish to produce and sell. So they push to gain flexibility and increase productivity as if, in the spirit of globalized competition, they were trying to maximize profits. If the employer can make more workers 'casual', fewer workers will work a standard work week, receive full benefits, have seniority rights, be union members or have control over their workload. In a broader sense, casualization is a way for employers to gain flexibility for themselves while increasing insecurity for workers. As well, with casualization employers can increase productivity by speeding up work, standardizing procedures, downsizing, multi-skilling, reducing services to the public and under-funding.

One of the most troubling aspects of the Taskforce's recommendations is the establishment of a "Transformation Incentive Fund" meant to ensure (among two other priorities), the `effective use of existing physical facilities' and `cost effective administration.' In other words, post-secondary institutions will comply with the industry-driven benchmarks, or be denied a portion of their funding for operating costs. There will be no labour representatives on committee to determine benchmarks and indicators. The "Incentive Fund" is similar to the coercive measures taken by the government in allocating operating costs on the basis of "performance". In the past two Ontario Budgets, the Conservative government has compelled Universities and Colleges to compete with one another for operating grants on the basis of market-driven criteria (e.g. student loan repayment rates; employment rates after graduation; graduation rates; ability to attract private investment partners; ability to attract private research money; efforts to contract-out services). In Budget year 2000-01, the government allocated some extra money for operating grant increases to Universities and Colleges based on their willingness and ability to accommodate enrolment increases. Last year, one third of universities got the largest amount of performance funding, the next third received less, and the bottom third received none at all, even though the difference between the "best" performer and the "worst" was only 10%. The differences in community colleges was even smaller and the effect highly arbitrary.

This government's "accountability" agenda was introduced into Ontario's post-secondary system last year when it first made a portion of operating grants contingent on meeting certain performance standards. It was refined through the work of the "Investing in Students" taskforce. Now, we are seeing the legislative aspect of this agenda which will bring us the "Public Sector Accountability Act" and the insertion of the so-called "Accountability Office" within the Ministry of Finance. The objectionable aspect of this agenda is the presumption that the public sector ought to be disciplined while the private sector can go about providing educational services in an unregulated manner. What kind of accountability is there in a privatized system? What are the implications for our equity goals? What kind of quality are we to expect as our post-secondary educational system is undermined in favour of a completely commercialized institution like the University of Phoenix which is, at present, advertising a "Summer Promo" in which you can save up to $250 if you register for your on-line degree by May 31st"?

Finally, the ideological aspect of state restructuring ought not to be overlooked. In the Budget Papers, public sector organizations have been redefined as "Transfer Partners" (Budget Paper F, p. 187). This new term allows the government to present public sector and private sector organisations as equally entitled to public funding.

Fightback strategies:

The Canadian Union of Public Employees represents 45,300 University workers across Canada, and holds 136 collective agreements with employers in the University sector. CUPE members work in a diverse range of occupational classifications, including trades, parking, maintenance, custodial, library, bookstore, foodservice, marker-grader, tutor, laboratory workers, administrative positions, lecturer and contract faculty. As a result, CUPE members are affected directly by the restructuring of the state and postsecondary education.

CUPE has consistently demanded that the federal government increase funding to the University sector. At our last Convention held in 1999, CUPE resolved to support a Youth Policy Statement calling for tuition freezes and decreases. Furthermore, CUPE resolved to:

- lobby universities and governments to actively recruit and fund women of all colours, visible minorities, the working class, gays and lesbians and people with disabilities for graduate study (res.179);
- lobby the federal and provincial governments to eliminate tuition fees for all undergraduate post-secondary degrees, diplomas and certificates (res.183);
- urge the federal government to take steps to ensure that no direct or indirect support is provided to private for-profit education and training institutions (res.184);
- demand that the federal government increase funding to hire additional CUPE positions in order to

reduce workload and subsequent burn-out (res.185)

Over the past year, CUPE members in the University sector have engaged in successful in fightback strategies through collective bargaining. In the summer of 2000, Local 3261 (part-time student workers at the University of Toronto Bookstore) were successful in preventing the employer from routing the Union and perpetuating their minimum wage policy. A first contract was achieved after a thirteen-week strike in which community allies offered crucial support for these young workers in their struggle. The University argued that it had no role to play in this conflict, but the Local was able to position their struggle in terms of the larger fight against privatization and corporate control in the University.

SCFP Local 2661 representing part-time lecturers at the Université du Québec à Trois-Rivières (UQTR) were victorious after months of struggle. First locked out in the summer of 2000, local 2661 went through a failed mediation process in the fall. They went out on strike between November 8 to January 9. Local 2661 was successful in negotiating substantial wage increases as well as computers and benefits. Salary scales now replace flat rate contracts for sessional lecturers. They will now be hired annually, rather than on a per-course basis. By June 2002, members will earn $46,079 to $54,340 to teach seven 3-unit courses. Wages will increase to as much as $60,066 by 2005, for 55 fulltime lecturers. This represents an increase of as much as 60%.

After an eleven week strike, members of CUPE 3903 at York University were successful in maintaining a clause protecting them from tuition increases. This victory has had an encouraging effect on the University sector paving the way for "tuition increase assistance' more generally. Local 3903 won breakthrough equality language, including a transsexual transition leave and benefits for International Students Health Insurance. The Local also negotiated increases bringing up the floor for the lowest paid members. Unit 3's first contract is a strong one that increases wages and benefits for graduate assistants, and incorporates the tuition indexation clause in their agreement as well.

On the eve of a strike at the end of January, CUPE Local 4600 members were successful in winning a new clause protecting University workers at Carleton University from 75% of every increase in tuition-fees. This is a significant victory, because it is a new clause in the collective agreement which goes a long way towards recognising teaching assistants, lecturers and contract faculty as University workers entitled to bargain benefits other University workers are entitled to. In the context of labour relations in Harris' Ontario, this is a breakthrough.

Respect, wages and job security were the issues for Local 3912 at Saint Mary's University this year. Local 3912 members at SMU celebrated a strong second contract with solid gains of workers rights, disability protection, course cancellation compensation, substantial raises in stipends, among others. Local 3912 members also work at Dalhousie and Mount Saint Vincent. Their negotiations have not yet been concluded. CUPE has gone into conciliation with Mount Saint Vincent University and Dalhousie. The main issues are money and job security. It was expected that these two Universities would accept the pattern set at Saint Mary's but they are refusing.

Conclusion

Privatization, from a union's perspective, is not an inevitable process. Nor is it necessarily the most efficient way to deliver services to the public. Neither is it self-evident that the private sector offers the highest quality services. In fact, we have watched the quality of service decline as the private sector has increased its control over service provision.

CUPE members have been studying privatization and they see the links between what goes on in their workplaces, at the bargaining table, in the community and across borders. Our struggles are influenced by years of underfunding, government restructuring and global regulation and CUPE remains "On The Line" with our brothers and sisters working in the University sector. ❖

Endnotes

1. www.cupe.ca
2. Canadian Union of Public Employees, Ontario Confederation of University Faculty Associations, Canadian Federation of Students, Media Release, "Parents worry about access to postsecondary education" May 7, 2001
3. CUPE Research, "A Comparison of the FTAA Draft Investment Chapter and NAFTA Chapter 11" April 23, 2001
4. http://www.cupe.ca/issues/privatization/arp/default.asp
5. [6. Notwithstanding paragraph 5, if an investor of a duly authorized Party provides services or performs functions of correctional services, income insurance or unemployment insurance or social security services, social welfare, public education, public training, health, and child care, the investments of that investor shall be protected by the provisions of this Chapter.]
6. [7. This Chapter applies to the entire territory of the Parties and to any level or order of government regardless of any inconsistent measure that may exist in legislation at those levels or orders of government.]
7. See Paul's Tables for exact figures
8. "Government Funding Cuts Hamper Access" CAUT News, Bulletin Online. September 2000.
9. Darren Stewart, "Student loans go private", Varsity News 121:6 December 4, 2000
10. Government of Canada, "The Budget plan 2000", p.108.
11. Canadian Association of University Teachers, "Commentary on Federal Budget 2000." www.caut.ca/English/Lobby/Budget_2000/commentary.htm March 3, 2000 pp.2-3.
12. Canada Foundation for Innovation, "Update on CFI activities", CFI home page, October 24, 2000 www.innovation.ca/english/programs/indexoct17.html
13. Question Period During the April 21 press conference, PM Jean Chretien. (29:46 minutes) www.americascanada.org/eventsummit/document/summit-e.asp

Big biotech buys the building: Students and faculty confront big money and corporate science on campus

By Lucy Sharratt

In 1993, at the York University Annual Awards Dinner, Richard Mahoney, then CEO and Chairman of Monsanto Company, was speaking about the collaboration of university researchers and the support to the biotechnology industry, both financial and otherwise, from the Canadian government.

"This focus and exercise of political will in biotechnology," he said, "has been an incredible achievement rarely if ever duplicated in peacetime."[1]

Federal, provincial, even regional and local governments are supporting the growth of the "Life Sciences" industry, giving money and infrastructure support to corporations investing in the new technologies of genetic engineering, all while cutting funding for research at universities. The result is a distinct lack of independent research, and growing controversy and conflicts inside university communities.

Biotechnology: A "Wall Street science"

"Knowledge is the key commodity in today's global economy, and university research is society's primary source of this knowledge."
—*President and Vice-Chancellor of the University of Manitoba Dr. Emoke Szathmary.*[2]

Genetically engineered foods, seeds and medicines were born in the university lab and grew up on Wall Street. Well-known author and critic of genetic engineering, Vandana Shiva, calls biotechnology a "Wall Street Science" because this is where, she argues, the real decisions are made about research and development.[3] By the early 1980s, biotechnology was an emerging industry, with its origins in university research. The links between university and industry are particularly strong in Life Sciences research because of the nature of the technology itself, the power of the corporations investing, and the poor state of public funding for universities.

The tremendous commercial potential of genetic technologies, the ability to patent "inventions," and the power of the corporations that have captured most of this wealth are defining features of the technology. A few large transnational agrochemical and pharmaceutical corporations dominate the development and marketing of genetically engineered seeds, foods and drugs, with the technologies also being applied to weapons manufacture and the forestry, fisheries and mining industries.

It is the grand promises of benefits in the public good, so far unrealized, that are used to justify charging ahead uncritically with biotechnology research and rushing to commercialize that research through partnerships with private companies. The result is a technology sped to market before democratic debate and before safety questions are fully and independently investigated.

Democracy (NOT!) and biotechnology

Biotechnology research forges ahead and products are emerging from campus research, but this research has never been subject to democratic and public debate in Canada, let alone inside the universities themselves. Indeed, pursuit of the technology in its many forms and stages of development is extraordinarily controversial. University researchers and administrations, however, have bought and sold the promise of biotechnology. And so universities now find themselves home to research in genetic engineering when there is no societal consensus on the usefulness and ethics of the technology, and where safety questions are unresolved.

University-corporate research in genetic engineering further entrenches biotechnology into our reluctant society. With biotech and biotech corporations establishing a significant presence on campus, the message communicated is that there is money in biotechnology, and the technology is here to stay.

There is tremendous money and power at stake in the future of biotechnology, and the corporations that stand to gain the most are desperate to maintain control over its direction. As Richard Mahoney of Monsanto argued, "The biotech race can be won—and I'm confident it will be—because it must be...Biotechnology is the battleground upon which all future technology battles will be fought."[4] Corporations like Monsanto are very clear that the university is one central field of this battleground.

The research agenda: research grants and industry partners

Research in genetic engineering is overwhelmingly directed towards the development of products for commercialization. One of the major reasons for this is the increasing reliance on industry money to fund research projects. Governments are responsible in large part for this situation, not just because they have cut funding to universities, but also because the majority of government granting programs actually require industry partnerships or matching funds from corporations (usually 50% and sometimes as high as 65%).

In 1997, the federal government established the Canadian Foundation for Innovation, with $800 million dollars, to "modernize" research infrastructure at universities across Canada. It requires researchers to find corporate partners for matching funds. CFI is at arm's length from the government, "to encourage the kind of collaboration and partnerships among research institutions and the private sector which are critical to making Canada competitive internationally."[5]

Through corporate funding, research is explicitly driven by expected commercial value rather than evaluation of, and negotiation over, social value. There is little money available for research into problem-solving based on shared knowledge that can be used and owned collectively, like methods in preventative medicine or organic agriculture. Research is instead directed towards creating products that can be patented and sold for private profit, like blockbuster drugs or herbicide-resistant crops. Because Canada has no agriculture or food policy to speak of, there is no public direction in research in this sector, so the research agenda is largely left to powerful corporate players in the industrial agriculture sector.

The translation of this into the university research community is an increasing deficit of curiosity-based research and a focus instead on research for products and profits. Funding in other disciplines is also suffering because of the focus on Life Sciences as the most promising technology for the new knowledge-based economy and the one that can be most immediately patented for profit.

Spin-off companies, spin-in profits?

Spin-off companies are becoming an established way to take basic research into stages of product development and commercialization. Through spin-off companies, university research is fed directly into the biotechnology industry. Spin-off companies are created to license technologies from the university.

Universities are increasingly creating more and more infrastructure to encourage and accommodate these spin-off companies. Many universities now have their own "technology transfer offices." At the University of Guelph, Technology Transfer Officer Sheldon Karwarsky states that the university is "strongly committed to providing a vigorous, aggressive program of commercial development of technologies arising from university research, both to increase university revenues and to contribute towards economic development in Ontario and Canada."[6]

One example of this type of spin-off is Performance Plants, a small biotechnology company that was founded in 1995 by two members of the plant biology group at Queen's University. The company headquarters are now located at the new $52.5 million dollar

Biosciences Complex on Queen's campus. The complex was built to house the university's spin-off companies and is home to the university's technology transfer office, PARTEQ Innovations Inc., which was instrumental in financing Performance Plants and in fact owns 12% of the company. "Many of the technologies of the company are derived from basic research done by Queen's scientists," states Dr. David Dennis, professor at Queen's for more than 25 years and founder and President of Performance Plants.

But the role of Performance Plants in the university community and beyond is not limited to research and product development; they are also active in "public education to highlight the positive attributes of genetically modified foods."[7]

University research parks: "Home Sweet Corporate Home"

University research parks are one very obvious way in which universities create space for private industry. The physical layout of universities now includes corporate offices, and the geography of the public space is intimately tied to the private.

- Syngenta has a "Crop Protection" or pesticide product sales office at the University of Guelph Research Park.
- Monsanto is a tenant at Innovation Place, a research park created by the Government of Saskatchewan and the University of Saskatchewan in 1977. The purpose of the research and development park "is to facilitate and encourage the creation of new jobs." It was designed "to encourage further applications of academic research where industry and the university could meet and work together."
- The University of Manitoba's "SMARTPark" will soon be home to an R&D centre (thanks to $25 million from the province) that will focus on creating "functional foods" or foods engineered for nutritional or medicinal reasons.

Through these research parks, provincial and local governments and universities invest in infrastructure for corporate development in the guise of community economic development.

Making campus home to corporations: "Glaxo-NOT-Welcome"

What happens when the corporate sponsor of your university becomes the centre of a very public controversy, a target of community resistance, and the centre of a public relations disaster? In 1997, a number of powerful pharmaceutical corporations, including the company Glaxo Wellcome, took the South African government to court for supplying the cheaper generic versions of their patented AIDs drugs. When students at Queen's wanted to act against this aggressive patent protection on the part of the drug companies, they only had to look across campus to the new $2.5 million dollar medical research centre funded in part by, and named after, the pharmaceutical giantGlaxo Wellcome. In 1998, Glaxo spent $1 million to establish the "Glaxo Wellcome Clinical Education Centre" at Queen's University in Kingston, Ontario. Glaxo (now Glaxo SmithKline) is a major international drug company that took in nearly $30 billion in revenues in 2000.

The corporation advertised its investment in Queen's as a part of its "ongoing commitment to improving health and saving lives through innovative research and education," but as far as the students at Queen's were concerned, the university was accepting "blood money" from a company that was actively preventing people in Africa from accessing life-prolonging drugs.

"We are proud to be a partner with Queen's on this important venture," Glaxo stated when the centre opened. But soon after, students held a rally on campus and staged a "die-in" where they declared "Glaxo-NOT-Welcome." Students occupied the principal's office and demanded that the university publicly and officially ask the company to drop its lawsuit, take the corporation's name off the centre, sever all connections with Glaxo, establish an independent Donation Ethics Committee, and network with other universities to lobby for "the necessary funding to ensure intellectual and moral independence."[8]

Glaxo has a presence on other campuses across Canada, including the University of Toronto's Mississauga campus where the company spent $700,000 to create the "Glaxo Wellcome Core Laboratory for Biotechnology Research". Glaxo is only one of many large pharmaceutical corporations developing genetic technologies and partnering with universities to support medical research.

Independent science at risk

Ties to corporations threaten independent science. As Martha Crouch explained, after she quit her esteemed work in biotechnology for research in organic agriculture, "I myself was fully participating in the agendas of agribusiness without realizing it: I consulted for big companies where members of the biotechnology team at two big companies, Monsanto and Dupont, were sitting on grant panels at the National Sciences Foundation, helping to decide how public money was spent. I published results as fast as my lab could generate them without considering the consequences. My closest colleagues were spread equally between academic and industry labs, doing indistinguishable kinds of research. And I did not question any of this."[9]

The Expert Panel of the Royal Society of Canada on the Future of Food Biotechnology raised the issue of increased commercialization of university research, concluding that "the co-opting of biotechnology science by commercial interests contributes to the general erosion of public confidence in the objectivity and independence of science behind the regulation of food biotechnology.[10] The Expert Panel considers this a serious public policy issue related to the public funding of independent scientific research at universities, and it can only be remedied by those in government who formulate and implement these public policies."

Conclusion

James Turk of the Canadian Association of University Teachers argues that, under the type and degree of corporate influence seen today over post-secondary institutions, "the basic role of universities in democratic society is at risk."[11] Perhaps the role of universities in our democratic society is at risk because our democracy itself is at risk.

But across the country, resistance inside university communities to the many manifestations of corporate influence is strong and growing. Students and faculty are challenging the corporatization of university spaces—from the food in the cafeteria and advertisements on washroom walls to the new laboratory equipment and biotechnology buildings.❖

Endnotes

[1] Mahoney, Richard, "Policy is What You Do, Not What You Say: Biotechnology: The Next Economic Thrust for North America," York University Annual Awards Dinner, Toronto, Ontario, Monsanto Company, St. Louis, Missouri, 16 February 1993. page 2.

[2] "Federal-Provincial Partnership Funding Announced for University of Manitoba SMARTpark Project," Winnipeg, Government of Manitoba, October 15, 1999.

[3] Vandana Shiva, "The Plunder of Nature," *Synthesis/Regeneration* 19, Spring, Gateway Green Alliance, St. Louis, Missouri. 1999.

[4] Mahoney, page 8-9.

[5] Finance Canada, Budget, 1997

[6] Contact Canada, Sheldon Karwarsky, Technology Transfer Manager, originally published in Canadian Biotechnology 2000

[7] Cattaneo, Claudia, "Ag Biotech firm puts performance in plants," National Post, 19 May 2001.

[8] Glaxo-Not-Welcome Petition, Coalition Against Corporate Globalization, Queen's University

[9] Crouch, Martha, "Confessions of a botonist", New Internationalist, Issue 217, March, 1991

[10] Expert Panel on the Future of Food Biotechnology, "Elements of Precaution: Recommendations for the Regulation of Food Biotechnology in Canada," The Royal Society of Canada, Ottawa, January 2001. page 217.

[11] Turk, James L., "Introduction – What Commercialization Means for Education," in James L. Turk, ed., *The Corporate Campus: Commercialization and the Dangers of Canada's Colleges and Universities*, A CAUT Series Title, James Lorimer and Company Ltd., Toronto, 2000. p3.

University competition: New trouble in the making

By Claire Polster

There is a subtle but important development taking place within Canadian universities that is a "missing piece" we should keep our eye on. It is the growth of competition between and within universities that is being spurred by recent federal initiatives, particularly the establishment of the Canada Foundation for Innovation (CFI) and the Canada Research Chairs Program (hereafter referred to as "the CRC").

This competition is of concern because of the ways in which it reorients universities' and academics' attention and efforts toward their own particular needs and interests and away from the needs and interests of the general public. It is also worrisome because of the ways in which it renders universities and academics more vulnerable to the desires and demands of government and the business community.

Competition within and between Canadian universities is not a new phenomenon. Our universities and academics have always competed informally, particularly for intangibles such as reputation that are both ends in themselves and means of attracting other valued resources such as professors, students, and donations. However, the establishment of the CFI and the CRC is transforming and intensifying university competition in at least three significant respects. First, as these institutions' programs are open to and applied to by academic institutions, as opposed to the professors within them, they turn our universities into direct competitors for federal research funds. Thus, for the first time at the national level, the material interests of each Canadian university are in direct conflict with the interests of all others.

CFI and CRC programs also alter university competition by making its outcome more consequential than ever before. In contrast to most federal research support programs that are open in nature, the amount of CFI and CRC funds for which universities may apply is based on universities' track records in obtaining sponsored research funds. As access to funds in the future becomes contingent on acquiring funds in the past, universities' research competitiveness takes on far greater importance than it would were each round of competition to begin afresh.

A third notable feature of CFI and CRC programs is the requirement that each university produce, and make public, a strategic plan which adjudicators take into consideration when making funding decisions. The effect (if not intention) of this requirement is to expand the scope of inter-university competition which is no longer restricted to particular research proposals or initiatives but extends into universities' general missions, as well as their long-term plans.

At the same time that they transform inter-university relations, CFI and CRC programs are also altering relations within individual universities. Given that the amount of funds for which they may apply is based on each university's entire research track record, these programs tie the interests of each academic within a university to those of all others in novel ways. This change is likely to affect the ways in which academics view their colleagues and relate to them, both formally and informally.

It is also further altering the ways in which university administrators are orienting to the academics in their institutions[1]. Increasingly, academics are not being seen, or seen only as unique individuals whose work is to be facilitated through a number of means and for a variety of ends. Rather, they are being seen as members of the institution's "research team" whose job is to enhance the university's overall research performance and thereby maintain, if not advance, the institution's standing within the national university system. Put differently, the relationship between administrators and academics is becoming far more instrumental, to the point where it may actually be reversed: as opposed to universities and administrations being the means of supporting academics' goals, academics are becoming the means of supporting administrative and institutional goals.

In this new competitive context, university administrators are adopting a number of practices to enhance the performance of the players on their research teams. They are increasing the encouragement and support they provide to faculty to submit grant applications. They are also revising the rewards they offer to academics in order to motivate them to become more "research active."

At York University, for example, the administration has not only instituted merit pay, but super-merit pay, to stimulate and reward academic performance. At the same time that they attempt to bolster the performance of regular team members, administrators are prioritizing the recruitment and retention of "top grant producers." They are offering, or approving offers of, a variety of incentives (including salary increases, lab and other equipment, reduced teaching loads, special appointments, etc.) to valued academics to entice them to stay at—and preferably to move to— their institutions.

These and other efforts to enhance university competitiveness are having, and will have, a number of harmful effects within individual universities and the Canadian university system. For instance, efforts to cultivate, attract, and retain "research stars" are imposing a number of new costs on universities, whether or not they become involved in bidding wars for these prized academics. At the same time, these efforts are undermining the morale of many ordinary academics who are not simply denied "star treatment" but are penalized by it, by having to take on greater teaching loads or make do with less research resources and other support services. These efforts are also eroding the strength of, and possibly support for, faculty associations, which may harm academics individually and collectively.

At the level of the university system, competition is promoting (and normalizing) the practice of raiding or poaching valued academics, which can destabilize institutions and inhibit their ability to engage in, and follow through on, various kinds of planning. Inter-university competition is also producing new alliances—and new forms of exclusion—among various universities, which consume considerable resources and fragment the interests and solidarity of the university community.

It is the public, however, that is likely to suffer most from the growing competition within and between universities. For the primary effect of this competition is to entice and compel individuals and institutions in our university system to put their particular interests ahead of those of the general public. For example, the premium placed by universities on research stars is leading many academics to think of themselves, and to behave, as entrepreneurs who continually seek the best employment deal in the academic marketplace. This shift costs the public in the sense that it raises the price of academic labour. More significantly, it costs them by eroding the academic profession's public service ethic and the multiple practices that preserve it (which have not only been beneficial for Canadian citizens, but have been the basis of their support for public universities and the academics who work within them).

Universities' interests in acquiring top grant producers are also leading them to place their own interests over and above those of other institutions and the communities that they serve. The poaching of valued academics from other institutions (which is reportedly on the rise) may undermine research programs and projects within the home university that are valuable to the general public. It may also seriously disrupt research networks and alliances that serve the needs of surrounding communities.

Further, as academics and institutions that prioritize the public interest are affected by the actions of others, their ability and willingness to sustain this priority may be diminished. They may end up adopting means that are not simply incompatible with their ends, but that ultimately displace them. Such defensive action will be all the more tragic, given that the number of winners in any competitive system is generally far smaller than the number of losers.

While the public, many academics, and many universities are unlikely to benefit from increased competition, two other groups do stand to gain from it: the federal government and the business community. The federal government benefits from increased competition in the sense that it decreases universities' resistance to infringements on their autonomy. For example, although CFI and CRC programs undermine university autonomy by requiring universities to produce strategic plans and by transferring to government significant power over key institutional matters such as hiring, few if any universities have been willing—let alone able— to mount collective resistance to these programs in the new competitive context.

The business community benefits from competition as it heightens universities' sensitivity and receptivity to its desires and needs. In an increasingly competitive funding environment, administrations and academics are looking for any "edge" to increase the likelihood that their applications will be accepted. Given the federal government's progressive incorporation of the business community and its values in the creation, formulation, and adjudication of support programs for university research, applicants for funding may not simply be directly required, but also indirectly pressured and/or motivated, to develop proposals (and even strategic plans) that more closely conform to the needs of particular industries and to the innovation agenda more generally.

In sum, increased competition within and between universities is transforming the relationships and allegiances among various groups that have an interest in academic research. As academics and universities have more to win and more to lose in the new funding environment, their own needs and interests are taking precedence over the needs of groups outside of the university. Further, their own needs and interests are, more than ever, shaping decisions about which external groups' needs and interests they will prioritize in their research and other activities. Thus, in a number of ways, intensified competition is helping to displace an already fragile public service ethic by a private service ethic in our universities. Given the many harmful implications of this development for the general public, the university system, and even the business community, it should be, and can be, resisted.

There are numerous steps that those opposed to intensified competition in our universities can take. They can press for reforms to those aspects of particular federal research support programs (such as CFI and CRC programs) that promote competition and entrepreneurialism in our universities. They can also call for reforms to those aspects of federal and provincial governments' general approach to university and academic research support that have similar effects, such as the persistent underfunding of core operations.

Another strategy is to resist, if not reverse, those measures inside our universities that promote hierarchy, élitism, and competition, such as merit pay, incentive pay, and various other perks that are designed to cultivate and reward research stars. This strategy can be complemented by efforts to strengthen old mechanisms (such as collective agreements) and to develop new ones (perhaps under the auspices of organizations such as the CAUT, AUCC, and various learned societies) that foster greater collectivism and collaboration within and between academic institutions.

Ultimately, however, those concerned about university competition must address the corporatization of our universities, which is the larger whole of which competition is but a part. A greater understanding of the ways in which competition both contributes and responds to this larger problem will be a valuable resource in overcoming it. ❖

Endnotes

[1] It is worth emphasizing that relationships between administrations and academics in Canadian universities have changed dramatically over the last thirty years. My point here is not that CFI and CRC programs initiate changes in relations between these two parties, but that they advance and transform them in some particular ways.

Excerpt from women's economic independence and security:
A federal/provincial/territorial strategic framework
Federal/provincial/territorial Ministers responsible for the status of women
March 2001

Section 2.1 Education and Training
(Page 10)

Access for and retention of girls and women at all levels of education, including the higher level, and all academic areas is one of the factors of their continued progress in professional activities. Nevertheless, it can be noted that girls are still concentrated in a limited number of fields of study.

—Declaration and Platform for Action, United Nations, 1996, p.48.

❖ ❖ ❖

Women at all levels of education have fewer earning from full-time, full-year employment than their male counterparts.

Nonetheless, the link between education and employability has long been recognized. More highly education people are less likely to be unemployed and tend to work more hours, to earn more per hour, and to rely less on government support programs. In 1996, among women aged 25 to 34, the labour force participation rate stood at 59% for women without a high school diploma, 74% for women with a high school diploma, and 90% for women with a university degree or diploma.

For recent immigrants, however, especially women, education does not expand job opportunities to the same extent as for people born in Canada. While the employment rate for women born in Canada ranged from 52% for those without a high school diploma to 86% for university graduates, it was only 58% for women who were recent immigrants and were university graduates.

In 1981, among people aged 20 to 29, the same proportion of women and men (37%) were post-secondary graduates. In 1996, the proportions were 51% of women and 42% of men. At the university level, from 1981 to 1996, the proportion of graduates among women aged 20 to 29 rose from 11% to 21%, while among men in the same age group it rose from 12% to 16%. In 1997, 58% of all university graduates in Canada were women.

For Aboriginal women, educational levels continue to be lower than for other Canadian women, but there has been some improvement: from 1986 to 1996, the proportion of Aboriginal women who were high school graduates rose from 9% to 11%, while among Aboriginal men it rose from 8% to 13%; the proportion of Aboriginal women who were college graduates rose from 15% to 21%, while among Aboriginal men it rose from 14% to 19%; last, the proportion of Aboriginal women who were university graduates rose from 2% to 5%, while among Aboriginal men it rose from 1% to 3%.

As for women immigrants, on average, they are more highly educated than Canadian-born women: in 1996, 31% of them were university graduates, compared with 21% of Canadian-born women; the proportion of women lacking high school diplomas was similar in both groups.

Dropping out of school is less common among girls than boys, but remains a cause of concern because of its effects and impact on women's labour force participation rate and poverty. According to a 1991 study, over a 40-year employment period, a women dropout will spend 23.2 years outside the labour force, while a male dropout will spend only 6.6 years outside the labour force.

Men still form the majority of students in engineering, applied science, mathematics, and physical sciences, while women are still more numerous in fields related to the social sciences, education and health. At university, however, women aged 20 to 29 have greater representation than previously in science and technology: 34% of graduates in these fields were women in 1996, up from 8% in 1986.

In 1997, women between the ages of 25 and 44 participated more than

---

Ivory towers: Feminist audits, selected indicators of the status of women in Canadian universities

Degrees granted
(% to women, 1996-97) 56.8%
Bachelor 58.5%
Master 50.9%
Ph.D. 33.9%

Full-time faculty
(% women, 1998-99) 26.2% (8,804)
Full Professor 13.7% (1,899)
Associate Professor 29.1% (3,491)
Other Ranks 43.8% (3,414)

Full-time faculty wage gap (1998-99)
Women's average earnings as % of men's, all subjects 85.7%
Women's average earnings as % of men's, all subjects, controlling for age 94.9%

Senior academic administrators (% women, 2000)
President 16.7%
Vice-President 17.2%
Dean 25.8%
Department Chair 23.3%

men (29% vs. 27%) in adult education and training.

Unemployed women have higher (28%) rates of participation in training than do men (21%). Similarly, employed women have higher (44%) rates of participation than do men (38%).

In contrast to training, overall, women are somewhat less likely than men to receive employer-sponsored training, indicating that they are more likely to pay for it themselves. And while the F/P/T (Federal/Provincial/Territorial) Economic Gender Equality Indicators show that their participation rate in employer-sponsored training was close to men's at 97% in 1993, women received substantially fewer hours of training time at only 68%.

Persons with fewer than eight years' education participated at a rate of 5%. By contrast, persons holding a university degree participated at a rate of 50%. Both males and females show this pattern of participation.

Women (14%) are more likely than men (9%) to take a course for personal interest reasons, which may account for their higher participation rate, overall. Personal interest training is often less expensive and of shorter duration than job or occupation-specific training. ❖

Student debt load
(average for 4-year program) $25,000

Recent graduate wage gap
(1995) 82.8%
Median salary, all disciplines, 5 years post Bachelor:
Women $29,000
Men $35,000

Canada research chairs (2001)

	Tier 1	Tier 2	All Chairs
Women	18	20	38
Men	157	73	230
% women	11.5%	27.4%	16.5%

SSHRC research funding
(% of dollars awarded to women PI's, 2000-01)
Standard Research Grants - 42.8%
Strategic Theme Grants - 42.7%

Pension gap
(all women in Canada, 1997) 60.9%
Average annual after-tax retirement income, all sources:
Women $14,200
Men $23,300

Compiled by Wendy Robbins, Humanities and Social Sciences Federation of Canada Women's Issues Network, Judy Stanley, PAR-L Strategic Research Network, and Rosemary Morgan, CAUT Status of Women Committee. http://www.hssfc.ca/english/policyandadvocacy/win/indicators-women.cfm

Resisting casualization: Contract academic staff mobilize

By Vicky Smallman

Much is being said these days about the impending shortage of faculty in Canada's universities. Even *Globe and Mail* columnist Jeffrey Simpson has observed that "Universities are passing through a critical period in which they must hire thousands and thousands of new faculty members" (*Globe and Mail,* February 1, 2001).

With enrolment on the rise and a significant percentage of the tenured professoriate approaching retirement, our universities face a considerable challenge.[1] According to Simpson, "If universities cannot meet this challenge, class sizes will rise, the country's research capacity will shrink, the learning environment will deteriorate, and Canada's competitive position will decline."

"Shortage," however, may not be the right word to describe the situation. After all, there are plenty of underemployed PhDs working in and outside of academia. For well over a decade, opportunities for newly-minted Canadian PhDs have been few and far between. Cost-conscious universities were reluctant to make the commitment that a tenure-stream appointment requires, and instead filled teaching requirements with part-time, per-course, and limited term positions. Many would-be academics chose other careers. But many others took the work there was, and accepted contingent status in the hopes that if they demonstrated a commitment to the profession and the institution, they just might land one of the coveted full-time positions.

Contingent academics quickly discovered that, after a few years of teaching on contract, it can be extremely difficult to move to a full-time position. Academic jobs are competitive, and you need a proven research record in order to succeed. Yet many contract academics are hired for teaching duties only. They receive no compensation or support for scholarly and professional activity, are not considered to be internal candidates for the purposes of research grant applications, and even have their library privileges cut off between contracts. Some try to make a living teaching at several different universities or colleges, making it more difficult to find time to research, write and publish.

In addition to this professional marginalization, contract faculty also have to deal with the perception amongst colleagues that they didn't cut it as "real" academics. The irony of slogging it out with piecemeal teaching is that, the more one is re-hired, the less one is perceived as an appropriate candidate for new positions when they do arise.

When these fabled faculty positions materialize in the next few years (if, that is, universities receive appropriate funding from governments to fill these expected gaps), how can we ensure that individuals who have been doing the bulk of undergraduate teaching[2] are treated fairly and have access to some of these appointments?

One of the solutions is to establish fair treatment for contract faculty through collective bargaining. Faculty associations affiliated with the Canadian Association of University Teachers (CAUT) represent contract academic staff at eighteen campuses; the Canadian Union of Public Employees (CUPE) represents part-time faculty at 15 universities, and the Fédération nationale des enseignants et enseignantes du Québec de la Confédération des syndicats nationaux (FNEEQ-CSN) represent contract faculty at 10 universities in Quebec. There are independent part-time faculty unions at the University of Ottawa, Concordia, and Simon Fraser. Although part-time faculty have been unionized on several campuses for a couple of decades, there has been a renewed effort to organize in the past few years.

Faculty unions in particular have begun to recognize the importance of uniting full- and part-time faculty. In the last two years, faculty associations at Bishop's, Wilfrid Laurier, Nipissing, and Acadia have successfully certified bargaining units for contract academic staff. The University of Prince Edward Island, one of the few non-unionized faculty associations, certified a joint unit of full- and part-time academic staff. This kind of organizing success is somewhat rare in today's labour climate. There are likely several contributing factors: a strong, three-decade history of collective bargaining among academic workers in Canada is a major factor, as is the profound acknowledgement by contract academic staff of their own exploitation and marginalization,

Contract academic staff have begun to mobilize in other ways. This year, Canadian academic labour activists joined with colleagues in the United States to mount a joint campaign on fair treatment of contingent faculty. The week-long campaign, called "Fair Employment Week," was initiated by a coalition of unions and associations across Canada and the United States to educate the public, policy-makers, and the campus community about the effect the exploitation of part-timers has on the integrity of post-secondary institutions.

The campaign was a success as a mobilizing tool for local associations, as a public education opportunity, and as a coalition-building exercise. The campaign was endorsed by all the national organizations representing academic workers at universities and colleges, as well as a host of provincial and local associations and unions. Contract faculty members in six provinces held Fair Employment Week events. UBC's sessionals kicked off their campaign by handing out cinnamon buns and coffee (and petitions) to students as they arrived on campus. University of Saskatchewan's CUPE local used Halloween pumpkins to illustrate the differences between full-time and sessional faculty salaries, and displayed a photo collage of sessional instructors. Other campuses held poster campaigns, asked students to sign postcards, set up information tables, and held social events for their contract faculty.

Wilfrid Laurier's new part-time bargaining unit used the week to solicit support for their first contract negotiations. Their display focused on the contrast between the value contract academic staff provide in teaching and research, and the value the university attributes to them in wages. According to organizer Jonathan Haxell, the contrast is stark: "On average, in courses taught by part-timers, students pay more per person for texts for the course than the university pays per student for their instruction." (*CAUT Bulletin*, November 2001.)

In addition to improved wages, access to benefits, and an end to arbitrary hiring processes, unionized contract academic staff have made some real progress toward recognition of their status as professionals and their important role in university education. Wilfrid Laurier's emphasis on contract academic staff research during Fair Employment Week certainly had a positive outcome. Their first collective agreement, ratified in December 2001, included professional expense reimbursements and a fund to support research activities. While this kind of language is not new to part-time faculty agreements, it is becoming more of a priority for academic workers who want to end the two-tiered approach to academic labour.

Service is also an important part of the academic career. Yet contract faculty are often excluded from university committees—if they can participate, they are rarely compensated for the committee work they do. The first contracts for the new part-tine units at Bishop's and Wilfrid Laurier both included language guaranteeing representation on university committees and governance structures. At Bishop's, they were able to negotiate stipends for members who are active in Faculty Association activities. Concordia's Part-Time Faculty Association negotiated an extensive system for compensating union activists and representatives on university committees.

These remedies are not substitutes for adjusting the workload of contract faculty to include scholarly and professional activity and service (and compensating them accordingly), but they are steps in the right direction. Certainly, these changes will help newer contract faculty compete for tenure-track positions when they do arise. And they address a concern among all faculty about the gradual unbundling of the academic career—the separation of research from teaching, the devaluing of collegial approach to university governance—a symptom of the corporate management culture that has infiltrated our campuses.

But, in addition to thinking about the big picture, we cannot ignore the significant number of people who have been teaching part-time for years, who have not been able to maintain the necessary publishing record because they were too busy eking out a living. In negotiating language that provides newer contract academic staff with access to a career path, we must take care not to negotiate others out of their jobs. Job security, right of first refusal, and conversion for people who have been repeatedly re-hired must also remain a priority.

Of course, securing improvements for contingent faculty and ensuring they have access to the full-time positions only go so far toward addressing the challenge of faculty renewal. The problem of dwindling funds to universities still exists, and unless governments begin to reinvest in universities' operating funds, the casualization of the academic profession will continue. ❖

Endnotes

[1] In Ontario, where changes to the secondary school system will result in the so-called "double cohort" of high school graduates, the challenge is even more pronounced. See "Less isn't More: Ontario's Faculty Shortage Crisis", Ontario Confederation of University Faculty Associations, Research Report Vol. 1, No. 4, January 2001.

[2] Accurate Canadian statistics for the percentage of undergraduate teaching performed by part-time and contract faculty are not available. In the US, part-time and non-tenure track faculty make up 60% of the professoriate. Anecdotal information and existing statisitics tell us that the situation is slightly better in Canada, but the trend is similar.

Appendix

Equity: Background research and statistics

Percentage Change International Student Participation Rate

Province	1997-98	MP3 Rank	MP2 Rank
NF	9.3%	5	n/a
PEI	30.0%	2	n/a
NS	11.9%	3	n/a
NB	30.8%	1	n/a
PQ	7.2%	7	n/a
ON	8.7%	6	n/a
MB	-4.7%	10	n/a
SK	11.3%	4	n/a
AB	6.7%	8	n/a
BC	1.9%	9	n/a

Source: Education in Canada 2000

Percentage of International University Students

Province	1998/99	MP3 Rank	MP2 Rank
NF	3.3%	10	9
PEI	3.6%	9	10
NS	6.2%	3	4
NB	4.7%	7	8
PQ	9.8%	1	3
ON	4.3%	8	5
MB	4.8%	4	2
SK	4.7%	6	7
AB	4.7%	5	5
BC	8.6%	2	1

Source: Education in Canada 2000

Women as a Percentage of Tenured University Faculty

Province	2000/01	MP3 Rank	MP2 Rank
NF	24.2%	8	10
PEI	26.1%	4	3
NS	32.4%	1	1
NB	28.0%	2	2
PQ	25.3%	5	9
ON	24.4%	6	8
MB	26.3%	3	6
SK	22.0%	9	5
AB	21.3%	10	7
BC	24.3%	7	4

Source: Statistics Canada as cited in Bulletin Vol. 48 No.8

Unemployment Rate*

Province	2001	MP3 Rank	MP2 Rank
NF	16.1%	10	10
PEI	11.9%	9	9
NS	9.7%	7	7
NB	11.2%	8	8
PQ	8.7%	6	6
ON	6.3%	4	1
MB	5.0%	2	2
SK	5.8%	3	4
AB	4.6%	1	3
BC	7.7%	5	5

Source: CansimII Labour Force Survey, Feb 2, 2002

* The use of provincial unemployment rates by no means implies that we agree with the tying of higher education funding or priorities to job market performance of graduates: we do, however, recognize the role and responsibility of provincial governments in ensuring that graduates are given the opportunity to use the education they have received.

Inequality Index

Province	1999	MP3 Rank	MP1 Rank
NF	0.90	10	10
PEI	0.82	9	7
NS	0.62	4	4
NB	0.77	8	9
PQ	0.72	6	8
ON	0.51	3	3
MB	0.70	5	5
SK	0.75	7	6
AB	0.43	2	1
BC	0.43	1	1

Calculated with StatsCan data found in Ed. Quarterly Review
% of population with less than secondary education compared with % of population with PSE

Quality: Background research and statistics

Percentage Change in Fulltime Faculty

Province	1998/99-1999/00	MP3 Rank	MP2 Rank
NF	0.0%	6	10
PEI	6.8%	1	1
NS	2.8%	3	5
NB	-3.1%	10	3
PQ	-0.8%	8	7
ON	0.1%	5	8
MB	-2.6%	9	9
SK	1.6%	4	6
AB	3.3%	2	4
BC	-0.5%	7	2

Source: Statistics Canada

University Student/Faculty Ratio

Province	1999/00	MP3 Rank	MP2 Rank
NF	17.1	3	2
PEI	15.8	1	1
NS	17.1	4	4
NB	19.2	6	5
PQ	19.2	7	8
ON	21.4	10	10
MB	16.4	2	3
SK	19.9	8	7
AB	20.5	9	10
BC	18.6	5	6

Source: Statistics Canada

Per Capita Provincial Expenditure on PSE

Province	2000/01	MP3 Rank	MP2 Rank
NF	$382	5	n/a
PEI	$282	10	n/a
NS	$324	8	n/a
NB	$375	6	n/a
PQ	$444	1	n/a
ON	$286	9	n/a
MB	$401	3	n/a
SK	$402	2	n/a
AB	$387	4	n/a
BC	$360	7	n/a

Source: Statistics Canada General Revenue

Percentage Change in Per Capita Expenditure

Province	1999/00-2000/01	MP3 Rank	MP2 Rank
NF	0.2%	4	n/a
PEI	-0.5%	6	n/a
NS	-5.4%	8	n/a
NB	-1.6%	7	n/a
PQ	-0.4%	5	n/a
ON	-9.0%	10	n/a
MB	3.3%	1	n/a
SK	2.0%	3	n/a
AB	-5.7%	9	n/a
BC	2.4%	2	n/a

CAUT Education Review, Vol. 3, No. 3

Provincial University Operating Grants Per Capita

Province	2000/01	MP3 Rank	MP2 Rank
NF	$233	2	1
PEI	$186	7	7
NS	$206	5	4
NB	$207	4	2
PQ	$236	1	5
ON	$143	10	10
MB	$207	4	3
SK	$187	6	6
AB	$176	8	8
BC	$172	9	9

CAUT Education Review, Vol. 3, No. 3

Percentage Change Provincial University Operating Grants

Province	1999/00-2000/01	MP3 Rank	MP2 Rank
NF	1.9%	4	n/a
PEI	3.0%	2	n/a
NS	-1.6%	10	n/a
NB	-1.4%	9	n/a
PQ	5.0%	1	n/a
ON	1.5%	5	n/a
MB	0.8%	8	n/a
SK	1.0%	7	n/a
AB	1.1%	6	n/a
BC	2.5%	3	n/a

CAUT Education Review, Vol. 3, No. 3

Accessibility, affordability and opportunity: Background research and statistics

Range of Ancillary fees for University Students*

	2001/02 Low	2001/02 High
NF	$640	$808
PEI	$415	n/a
NS	$196	$607
NB	$108	$225
PQ	$40	$1,395
ON	$55	$894
MB	$130	$608
SK	$302	$788
AB	$133	$644
BC	$24	$435

Source: Statistics Canada

Average Undergraduate University Tuition Fees

Province	2001/02	MP3 Rank	MP2 Rank
NF	$2,970	4	4
PEI	$3,690	5	6
NS	$4,732	10	10
NB	$3,779	6	7
PQ	$1,912	1	1
ON	$4,062	9	9
MB	$2,795	3	3
SK	$3,831	7	5
AB	$3,970	8	8
BC	$2,465	2	2

The Daily, August 27, 2001

Percentage Yr-to-Yr Change in University Tuition Fees

Province	2000/01-2001/02	MP3 Rank	MP2 Rank
NF	-10.0%	1	n/a
PEI	6.0%	8	n/a
NS	4.9%	7	n/a
NB	7.4%	9	n/a
PQ	1.6%	4	n/a
ON	2.3%	5	n/a
MB	0.1%	3	n/a
SK	12.4%	10	n/a
AB	3.4%	6	n/a
BC	-2.2%	2	n/a

Source: Statistics Canada

*These figures are not included in the rankings.

Range of Tuition Fees for Canadian University Students*

	2001/02 Low	2001/02 High
NF	$2,970	$6,250
PEI	$3,690	$4,059
NS	$4,100	$8,150
NB	$3,290	$5,000
PQ	$1,668	$5,402
ON	$2,600	$15,680
MB	$2,692	$12,236
SK	$3,300	$32,000
AB	$3,470	$14,737
BC	$2,181	$11,070

Source: Statistics Canada

Average College Tuition Fees

Province	2001/02	MP3 Rank	MP2 Rank
NF	$1,452	4	4
PEI	$2,000	7	8
NS	$1,950	6	2
NB	$2,400	8	10
PQ	$0	1	1
ON	$1,752	5	5
MB	$1,298	3	3
SK	$2,442	9	9
AB	$2,601	10	6
BC	$1,273	2	7

Source: Department of Advanced Education, Manitoba

Percentage Yr-to-Yr Change in College Tuition Fees

Province	2000/01-2001/02	MP3 Rank	MP2 Rank
NF	0.0%	6	n/a
PEI	0.0%	6	n/a
NS	11.4%	10	n/a
NB	0.0%	6	n/a
PQ	0.0%	6	n/a
ON	2.0%	7	n/a
MB	0.0%	6	n/a
SK	9.0%	8	n/a
AB	11.2%	9	n/a
BC	-5.0%	1	n/a

Source: Department of Advanced Education, Manitoba

Percentage Change in University Tuition Fees

Province	1991/92-2001/02	MP3 Rank	MP2 Rank
NF	92.4%	6	9
PEI	74.1%	4	3
NS	115.0%	8	7
NB	87.0%	5	2
PQ	46.2%	2	5
ON	127.6%	9	8
MB	61.1%	3	4
SK	111.4%	7	6
AB	160.8%	10	10
BC	29.0%	1	1

Source: Statistics Canada

Percentage Change in College Tuition Fees

Province	1991/92-2001/02	MP3 Rank	MP2 Rank
NF	161.2%	7	9
PEI	62.6%	3	4
NS	154.2%	6	2
NB	300.0%	10	10
PQ	0.0%	1	1
ON	119.0%	5	5
MB	88.1%	4	6
SK	201.5%	8	8
AB	292.9%	9	9
BC	11.2%	2	3

Source: Department of Advanced Education, Manitoba

PSE Participation Rate (18-24 yrs)

Province	1998/99	MP3 Rank
NF	33.4%	4
PEI	32.6%	5
NS	42.2%	2
NB	32.0%	6
PQ	43.1%	1
ON	35.7%	3
MB	22.9%	10
SK	25.5%	8
AB	28.8%	7
BC	24.7%	9

Source: Education in Canada 2000

Percentage Change in PSE Participation Rate 1997/98 to 1998/99*

Province	% change
NF	6.4%
PEI	9.4%
NS	0.7%
NB	2.6%
PQ	-0.5%
ON	0.3%
MB	1.3%
SK	-3.4%
AB	-1.0%
BC	2.5%

Source: Education in Canada 2000

*These figures are not included in the rankings.

Missing Pieces III

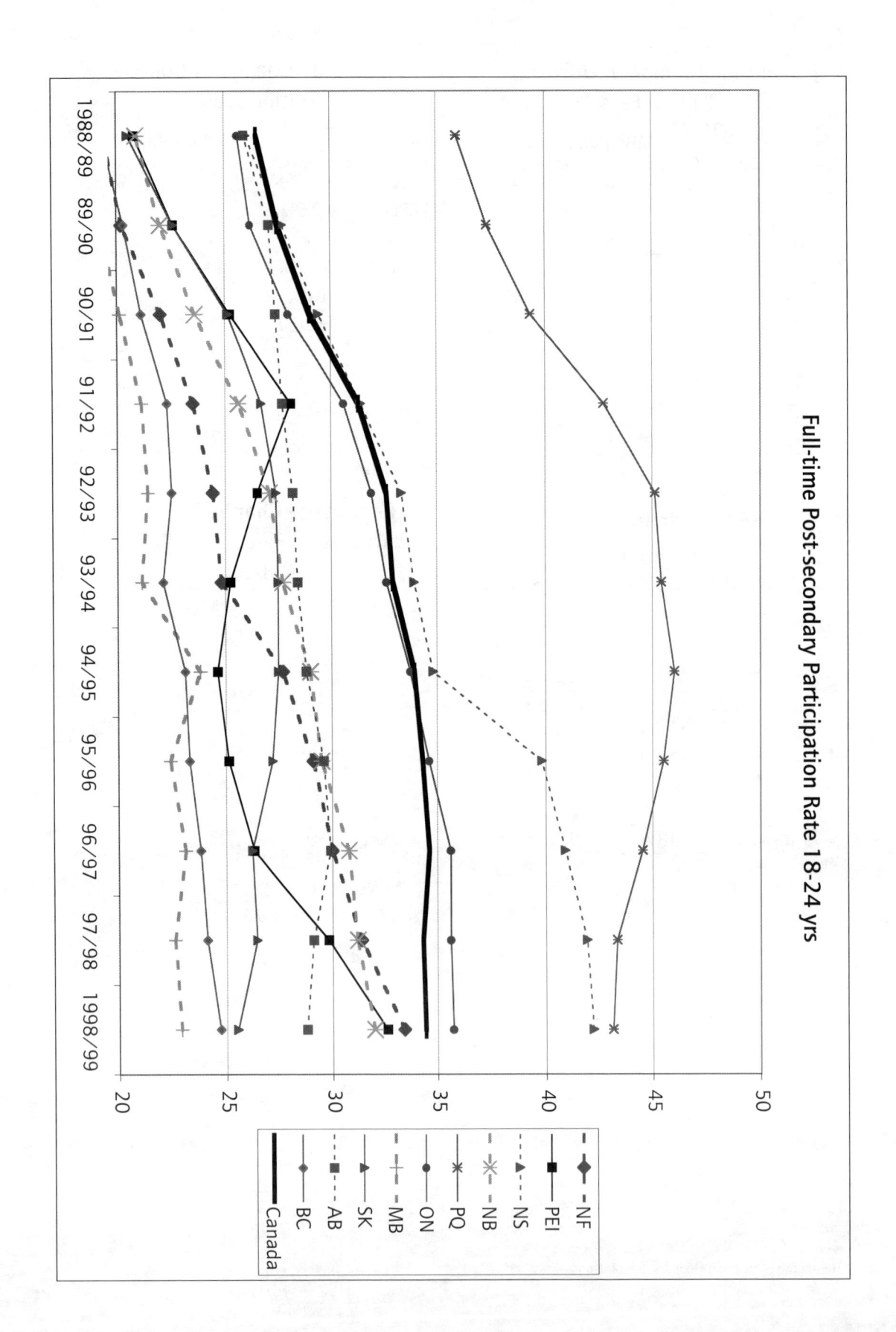

Full-time Post-secondary Participation Rate 18-24 yrs

144 Canadian Centre for Policy Alternatives

Public accountability: Background research and statistics

Percentage of Total PSE Budget Received from Student Fees

Province	1999/00	MP3 Rank	MP2 Rank
NF	20.0%	6	6
PEI	22.3%	7	7
NS	25.5%	10	10
NB	22.5%	8	8
PQ	11.9%	1	1
ON	24.1%	9	9
MB	18.2%	5	4
SK	15.9%	2	2
AB	17.5%	4	5
BC	17.3%	3	3

Source: The Daily, July 30, 2001

Percentage of Total PSE Budget Received from Government Grants

Province	1999/00	MP3 Rank	MP2 Rank
NF	62.2%	2	2
PEI	55.1%	7	3
NS	43.4%	10	10
NB	52.6%	8	8
PQ	65.3%	1	1
ON	49.4%	9	9
MB	58.5%	3	4
SK	57.3%	4	5
AB	55.1%	7	7
BC	55.2%	5	6

Source: The Daily, July 30, 2001

Percentage of Total PSE Budget Received from Private Sources

Province	1999/00	MP3 Rank	MP2 Rank
NF	3.7%	2	1
PEI	3.3%	1	2
NS	7.8%	6	3
NB	5.6%	3	5
PQ	10.4%	9	8
ON	10.9%	10	10
MB	9.3%	8	9
SK	7.1%	5	6
AB	9.0%	7	7
BC	6.5%	4	4

Source: The Daily, July 30, 2001

Educational attainment - Percentage aged 25+ with PSE

Province	1999	MP3 Rank	MP2 Rank
NF	42.6%	9	n/a
PEI	43.8%	7	n/a
NS	49.5%	2	n/a
NB	42.8%	8	n/a
PQ	45.7%	5	n/a
ON	47.6%	4	n/a
MB	44.0%	6	n/a
SK	41.9%	10	n/a
AB	50.3%	1	n/a
BC	48.1%	3	n/a

Education Quarterly Review

After High School 18-20 year old PSE Continuers

Province	1999	MP3 Rank	MP2 Rank
NF	54.3%	3	n/a
PEI	51.2%	4	n/a
NS	57.8%	2	n/a
NB	50.1%	6	n/a
PQ	62.3%	1	n/a
ON	48.7%	7	n/a
MB	44.4%	9	n/a
SK	46.4%	8	n/a
AB	42.1%	10	n/a
BC	50.5%	5	n/a

Statistics Canada, At A Crossroads, January 2002.

Missing Pieces III

Needs-based assessment by province 2000-2001

Province	univ. tuition fee freeze/rollback	college tuition fee freeze/rollback	needs-based grants program	loan remission/debt reduction	**MP3 Rank**	MP2 Rank
NF	2	1	-	1	**4**	8
PEI	-	1	1	1	**6**	6
NS	-	-	-	-	**10**	10
NB	-	1	1	1	**6**	6
PQ	1	2	1	1	**2**	6
ON	-	-	-	1	**9**	10
MB	1	1	1	1	**4**	1
SK	-	-	1	1	**8**	6
AB	-	-	1	1	**8**	8
BC	2	2	1	1	**1**	1